Stir-fry!

Stir-fry!

Fresh and tasty recipes for your wok and skillet

Katie Rogers

Good Books

Intercourse, PA 17534
800/762-7171
www.GoodBooks.com

Dedication
To Megan and Thomas

International Standard Book Number: 978-1-56148-595-6 (paperback edition)
International Standard Book Number: 978-1-56148-596-3 (comb-bound edition)
Library of Congress Catalog Card Number: 2007009141

Library of Congress Cataloging-in-Publication Data
Rogers, Katie.
  Stir-fry! : fresh and tasty recipes for your wok and skillet / Katie Rogers.
      p. cm.
Includes index.
  ISBN 978-1-56148-595-6 (pbk. : alk. paper) -- ISBN 978-1-56148-596-3
(comb-bound : alk. paper) 1. Stir frying. I. Title.
  TX689.5.R64 2007
  641.7'74--dc22
                        2007009141

Editor: Ruth Hamilton
Copy Editor: Anna Bennett
Design: Paul Wright
Photography: Stuart West
Food Styling: Katie Rogers
Production: Hazel Kirkman
Editorial Direction: Rosemary Wilkinson

Reproduction by Pica Digital PTE Ltd, Singapore
Printed and bound by C & C Offset Printing Co, China

Acknowledgments
Many thanks to my children, Meg and Thomas, for their constant support and willingness to try any recipe I serve them. To my partner Daniel for putting up with late nights in front of the stove. And finally, thank you to Stuart West for the fantastic photography in this book.

Contents

Introduction

The beauty of stir-frying is that it is quick, healthy and, if you cook using only ingredients in season, extremely economical. The wok is a great way of using up leftovers from the weekend, allowing you to create simple and delicious meals in moments for the rest of the week.

With everybody leading such busy lives, it's often hard to find the time to prepare and cook an evening meal. Fast food and ready-prepared meals tempt us away from the kitchen, to the extent that families rarely sit down and eat a meal together.

The purpose of this book is to make cooking easy and fun for everybody and to provide a few new ideas on how to combine simple flavors that you may never have thought of, as well as a few tips on how to shop intelligently and seasonally.

Each recipe is made with fresh ingredients. Selecting and buying the best and freshest ingredients should be very high on your priority list. Unfortunately, we are

conditioned to view shopping as a chore at the end of a long tiring day or week. Because of this, we are encouraged to shop in bulk from our local supermarkets. This means we over-shop and end up with many ingredients that just spoil in the fridge.

Cooking should be simple and stress-free, so every effort has been made to keep the number of ingredients and complicated techniques to a minimum.

Stir-frying, by its very nature, is an extremely quick method of cooking, so all the recipes in this book can be prepared in 30 minutes or less. This is often less time than it takes to heat a ready-prepared meal.

You will also find quick-cook adaptations of slow-cook classics such as Stir-fried beef chilli (page 44) and a warming Steak and mushroom goulash (page 45).

The equipment needed for stir-frying is minimal, which makes it a perfect cooking method for the smaller kitchen.

All you need is a wok (which needn't be expensive), a good sharp knife and a cutting board to create delicious, healthy meals.

Once you've mastered the art of stir-frying and have learned how different ingredients work together, you can begin to create your own stir-fry wonders!

Equipment

The great thing about stir-frying is you do not need a lot of equipment, so it is ideal for the busy cook or those with small kitchens. The wok originated in China thousands of years ago as a circular, round-bottomed, all-purpose cooking vessel. It was designed to be used over an open fire, so a gas stove is ideal. However, many modern woks now have flattened bottoms, making them equally efficient on electric stoves. Many woks also come with a steel ring, which helps to keep it steady.

BUYING A WOK OR FRYING PAN

You will find a huge range of woks available in stores today but which one you buy depends on your budget, and whether you cook on an electric or gas stove. If you don't want to buy a wok a large, non-stick frying pan will also work.

There are many woks to choose from, ranging from non-stick woks to round-bottomed, flat-bottomed, double-handled and single-handled ones. If you are a traditionalist, you may want to go for a cheap carbon-steel wok from your local Chinese specialty shop. They are a very good value but take a lot of looking after and "seasoning" (see page 22). Try and find a carbon-steel wok with a round base and a long wooden handle. The best size is about 14in (35cm). These work well on a gas stove, as this is the quickest heat source.

The double-handled wok is more popular than the single-handled type. It sets over your stove with an adapter ring under it to hold it in place. Any tossing is difficult with a double-handled wok, however. Single-handled woks are excellent for tossing the ingredients. The long handle gives you good leverage for flipping the wok and tossing the food inside.

KNIVES

Knives are really important and essential for a good working kitchen. Choosing a knife is a matter of personal preference, based on how comfortable the knife feels in your hand. Check that the weight and size feel right for you.

Carbon-steel knives are easy to sharpen and stay sharp for a long time. They rust easily, however, so must be wiped clean and dried immediately after use. Stainless-steel knives do not rust and can be used on highly acidic food. Unfortunately, they are difficult to keep sharp. High-carbon stainless-steel knives are ideal, as they don't rust and do stay sharp, but they are expensive.

Make sure your knives stay sharp by storing them either in a knife rack or on a magnetic strip on the wall. Do not store knives in drawers where the blade will be knocked.

FOOD PROCESSORS
A food processor is an essential piece of equipment and a good time-saver for the stir-fry cook! You can use it to chop, slice, grate and shred vegetables, a great asset when preparing a variety of different vegetables for a stir-fry. Small, compact processors that take up very little room are widely available and are not that expensive.

CUTTING BOARDS
I like large, thick, wooden boards, but plastic boards are hygienic and can be cleaned with an anti-bacterial cleaner. It's good to have one cutting board for raw foods, one for cooked foods and one for vegetables. The easiest way to do this is to buy three separate boards, all in different colors.

SPOONS AND SPATULAS
The Chinese spatula is specially designed for stir-frying. The edge of the spatula is rounded to fit the shape of the pan, and the utensil is sturdy, allowing stirring and tossing of large quantities of food.

An assortment of wooden or plastic spoons is also handy when cooking with a non-stick wok or frying pan.

SPICE GRINDER
This grinds whole spices to a fine or coarse power. If you can't find a spice grinder, a coffee grinder will work just as well.

VEGETABLE PEELER
Find a double-sided vegetable peeler, which is perfect for thinly slicing carrots, potatoes, celeriac and so on. Vegetable peelers are cheap, but I would use a stainless steel peeler – it is a lot more robust than its plastic relative.

Important ingredients

OILS

Different oils have different uses and some are more suitable for stir-frying than others.

Peanut and vegetable oils are good for stir-frying, as they can be cooked to a higher temperature than cold-pressed oils such as hemp oil.

For salad dressings and seasoning, buy a good-quality, single-estate, extra-virgin olive oil and sesame oil. If you want to start experimenting with other oils, try nut oils such as walnut or hazelnut. They have a delicious flavor but are more expensive, so buy in small amounts.

Peanut oil
Also known as groundnut oil, this is a good oil for frying and can be heated to a high temperature. I prefer peanut to vegetable oil as it has a mild flavor and is good for salad dressings.

Olive oil
If you cook with olive oil, make sure it's over a low heat. Olive oil burns at a very low temperature so is not ideal for intense frying at very high temperatures. Keep a cheaper olive oil for cooking and have a bottle of extra-virgin olive oil for seasoning at the end of a dish or for salad dressings.

Sesame oil
Use this sparingly as it has a very strong flavor. Sesame oil is not suitable for frying, so add at the end of cooking as a seasoning. Also great in Asian salad dressings.

Flavored oils
Again, use at the end of cooking to add an exciting kick to your dish. Also great in dressings.

Hemp oil
Originally a health-food staple used purely as a supplement, hemp oil has now moved into the kitchen and has a nutty flavor. Used in the same way as olive oil, it is a cold-pressed oil and is high in Omega 3 fatty acids. It's great used in salads.

NOODLES
Unless you are willing to make your own, fresh noodles should

only be bought from specialist Asian stores. The most commonly available ones in supermarkets are the dried version. They work just as well as the fresh variety and are not at all inferior. As with pasta, dried noodles work better in certain dishes than fresh ones do.

Cellophane noodles
These are made from mung beans and are also called glass noodles, bean thread noodles, bean vermicelli or slippery noodles. They work in soups, stir-fries and are also good deep-fried. They don't need cooking; just soak in boiling water to soften, drain and sprinkle with sesame oil.

Egg noodles
Fresh or dry, egg noodles come in a variety of shapes and sizes. They are the most common noodles in China and have a very distinctive flavor. They work best in meatier dishes, but are also good in soups and stir-fries. Fresh egg noodles should be boiled for 2–4 minutes; dried noodles 4–6 minutes.

Rice noodles
Made from rice flour and water, rice noodles work well in more delicate Thai dishes. They are wide and flat and pair well with saucy curries, such as the classic Thai green chicken curry (see page 27). Rice noodles are also good in soups, stir-fries and for deep-frying. Soak in hot water to soften for 15–20 minutes. Drain and run under cold water. This stops them from continuing to cook.

Rice stick noodles

Rice sticks are a thinner version of rice noodles. These noodles are used in the classic Pad Thai dish (see page 34). They are also used a lot in Vietnamese cooking and work brilliantly in stir-fries. Prepare in exactly the same way as rice noodles.

Wheat noodles

These have a very distinctive nutty flavor and are made from wheat flour and water. To cook fresh noodles, place in boiling water for 3–5 minutes. For dried wheat noodles, cook in boiling water for 5–8 minutes.

RICE
Basmati

Found mainly in Indian cooking, this rice is also ideal for any recipe that calls for a fluffy rice. It has a lovely nutty flavor and is perfect for pilafs due to its low starch content.

Arborio or carnaroli

This medium-grain rice contains its starch on the surface of the grain so that, when cooked, it creates a creamy consistency – ideal for risotto. Carnaroli is considered to be a superior risotto rice as it produces a creamier risotto. It is used a lot in Italian cooking.

Short-grain

This is probably the most versatile rice as it can be used for a variety of dishes, both savory and sweet.

Jasmine

This sticky, fragrant rice is very popular in Chinese, Vietnamese and Thai-style dishes. It has a high starch content, which means that the grains stick together, making it perfect to eat with chopsticks.

Long-grain

Long-grain rice is the most popular rice used in cooking as it absorbs well and is not as expensive as basmati rice. It is not as low in starch as basmati, but it still works well in most rice dishes.

PASTA

Pasta is an essential in any pantry. There are reportedly some 500 different shapes of pasta, and some are particularly suited to certain types of sauces. I have selected the types I think are most useful to have in your cupboard.

Fettuccine, pappardelle

These are wide-ribboned pastas that are made to go with robust, cream-based, meaty or rich tomato sauces.

Spaghetti, linguine

These are great for thin or oil-based sauces that will evenly coat the pasta. They are also suited to seafood-based sauces such as clams and mussels and work well with simple flavors such as herbs, garlic and olive oil.

Maccheroni, orecchiette

These are short pastas that are ideal for combining with chunky vegetable sauces that contain broccoli, beans and so on. Short pasta is also great to include in soups, stews and broths.

Penne, rigatoni

These are round in shape, with or without ridges. They are easily coated and are good with meat-, tomato- or cheese-based sauces.

COUSCOUS

Couscous, in my opinion, is a wonder food. In moments you can whip up a fragrant couscous salad with olives, parsley, feta and red onions dressed with a drizzle of olive oil and a squeeze of lemon. It also works well simmered in hot vegetable stock and is a perfect accompaniment to a meaty dish or rich vegetable stew. It's extremely cheap and a perfect staple in any busy cook's kitchen.

BULGUR WHEAT

Bulgur wheat can be used as an alternative to rice or couscous but has a higher nutritional value. Best known as the main ingredient in tabbouleh salad, bulgur is also a tasty, low-fat ingredient that can be used in pilafs, soups and stuffings. Because of its nutritional value and versatility, it is an ideal food in a vegetarian diet.

HERBS

Herbs are a great way of flavoring all kinds of dishes. The more robust herbs such as thyme, rosemary and sage work much better with fats and should be added to oils at the beginning or halfway through cooking. Softer herbs such as basil, cilantro and parsley have a higher water content and should always be added at the end of cooking; otherwise, they will lose all their flavor.

Fresh herbs are widely available from supermarkets, and if you can grow a pot on your kitchen windowsill – even better! They are easy to grow as long as you keep them well watered, in the sunlight and away from any harsh winds.

If you've bought packaged herbs or fresh bunches from your local greengrocer or deli, rinse in cold water, shake gently and store in a sealed plastic container at the bottom of the fridge.

To chop fresh herbs, use a sharp knife, hold the point steady on the cutting board with one hand and move the blade around in a wide arc with the other, chopping as you go.

If you can only get hold of dried herbs, I would stick to oregano, rosemary and thyme. Try to find leaves rather than the chopped variety, and buy in small quantities as they lose their aroma and flavor over time. Always add dried herbs to dishes that are to be cooked rather than using them in uncooked dishes such as dressings and salads.

Basil
With its unique aroma and aniseed flavor, basil is one of the best-loved and most popularly grown herbs in the world. We associate basil with Italian cooking but it actually originated in the Far East and is used a lot in Asian cooking.

Oregano
Very closely related to marjoram, oregano is grown in the Mediterranean and is very popular in Greek cooking. For the best flavor, add fresh oregano in the last few minutes of cooking. It can go bitter if you cook it too long. Add to salads, casseroles or sauces; it is particularly good in chicken dishes. Dried oregano works very well in tomato-based dishes.

Mint
Distantly related to basil and part of the aniseed family, mint is associated with English cooking – especially in mint sauce served with lamb. However, it is widely used throughout the world and is an essential ingredient in many Lebanese, Greek and North African recipes.

Cilantro
With its pungent and distinctive flavor, cilantro cannot be confused with any other herb. Its unique

flavor works very well with Indian and Asian dishes and is great sprinkled over salads.

Flat-leaf parsley

Considered more flavorsome than the curly variety, flat-leaf parsley has a milder taste and is incredibly versatile. It can be used for pestos and dressings, and also makes a good alternative to cilantro for garnishing Indian and Asian dishes.

Dill

This Scandinavian favorite is the perfect partner for fish. The silky green fronds have a flavor similar to caraway. Dill is also widely used in Greece and the seeds are used in the classic spinach, feta and filo pie. Add at the end of cooking.

Lemongrass

This is a tall, lemon-scented Asian grass that is used mainly in Thai cooking. Peel away the outer leaves and use the tender root in the center. Chop finely and use to infuse flavor into a dish; but remove before serving. Lemongrass works well in sweet dishes too. It is now widely available in Asian shops and major supermarkets.

Rosemary, thyme and sage

These are all harder shrub herbs that are best added at the beginning of cooking. They are good for flavoring oils and work well with strong sauces and heavier meat dishes.

SPICES

Spices such as cumin, coriander, cinnamon or cloves add flavor and depth to the simplest of meals. Buy in small quantities as they lose their flavor and fragrance very quickly – it is also a good idea to store them in an airtight container in a dark, cool place. Whole spices need to be dry-roasted before adding to a dish so that the essential oils are released (along with the flavors). Simply place in a hot, dry pan until they start to smoke.

VINEGARS

Vinegar is used to make pickles, de-glaze pans, marinate meats and add a lovely tang to vinaigrettes, sauces and even desserts. Keep a bottle of white-wine vinegar on hand if you can – it works well in a number of dishes and has a lovely mellow flavor, perfect for cooking with. Also keep a bottle of balsamic vinegar in your pantry at all times. This lovely sweet vinegar is perfect for dressings, marinades or simply for sprinkling over meat and vegetables when cooking a stir-fry.

Unopened, most vinegars will last for about two years in a cool, dark pantry. Once opened, vinegar should be used within three to six months.

NUTS AND SEEDS

Shelled nuts are best kept sealed in the fridge in hot weather. This will prevent the oils in the nuts from going rancid.

You can enhance the flavor of nuts and seeds by placing them in a single layer on a baking sheet. Cook in the oven for about 10 minutes at 350°F (180°C) until they turn golden and become fragrant. Alternatively, heat a small, heavy-based frying pan and dry-fry them.

Sesame, poppy, mustard and pumpkin seeds are good to have in small quantities. To bring out their flavor, heat in very hot oil for about 30 seconds. Remove or add other ingredients to prevent them burning in the oil.

SAUCES, PESTOS AND PASTES
Thai red and green curry paste
These have become increasingly popular. Despite its color, red curry paste is milder than green. Red curry paste is made from ground red chillies, garlic, lemongrass, shrimp paste and ginger. Green curry paste is made from hot green chillies, coriander, cilantro and lemongrass. With the addition of coconut cream, they make wonderful fragrant curries.

Fish sauce (*nam pla*)
This is a clear, amber liquid that is drained from salted, fermented fish. It is used as a flavoring and seasoning in Thai cooking and is available from Asian shops and supermarkets.

Oyster sauce
Commonly used in Chinese and Filipino cuisine, this is a dark brown sauce originally prepared from oysters. It often contains flavor enhancers such as monosodium glutamate. Buy an oyster sauce made with oyster extract.

Hoisin sauce
A thick, sweet-tasting Chinese sauce made from fermented soybeans, sugar, salt and red rice. It can be used as a dipping sauce or as a glaze for pork dishes and works well in stir-fries made with red meats such as lamb and beef.

Sweet chilli sauce
Great for adding a little heat to any dish, sweet chilli sauce is a mixture of ground chillies, shrimp paste and tamarind. It also works well as a dipping sauce.

Harissa paste
This hot and spicy paste made with red chillies, garlic, spices and olive oil originates in North Africa and is used as an accompaniment to couscous dishes. Harissas vary in heat so find one that suits your palate.

Passata and canned tomatoes

Invaluable in any kitchen, passata is a smooth tomato sauce that has been sieved. It's perfect for making sauces to add to pasta. Canned tomatoes are an excellent ingredient as they have a robust, concentrated flavor that even fresh tomatoes often lack – this is because they have been canned immediately after picking. Use as a base for soups and sauces and summer stews.

Soy sauce

Soy or soya sauce is a fermented sauce made from soybeans, roasted grain, water and salt. Originally from China, it is now popular all over the world.

Virtually all soy sauce has some alcohol added during bottling, which acts as a preservative. This means that soy sauce should always be kept in the fridge out of direct light, otherwise it could taste slightly bitter.

Pesto

This is the signature sauce of Ligurian cuisine, originally made to preserve the summer crop of basil throughout the winter. Pesto recipes vary from cook to cook but the main ingredients are herbs, such as basil or flat-leaf parsley, garlic, olive oil, pine nuts and cheese. Once you've mastered the art of making a pesto, you can start experimenting with different ingredients. I like hazelnut pesto with cilantro and goat's cheese.

If you don't want to make your own, there are now many good pestos available from supermarkets or even homemade ones in local delis. Always keep a couple of jars in your pantry to spice up vegetables, pasta sauces or steamed potatoes.

OTHER PANTRY ESSENTIALS
Mustards

Mustard pastes are made from ground mustard seeds blended with oil and vinegar. They come in different strengths and add a great flavor kick to food. I tend to use a mild-strength mustard, such as French Dijon mustard, for general cooking. For a fiery kick, use a strong English mustard. If you want to give your sauces a grainy texture, add a wholegrain or seeded mustard.

Anchovies and capers

These are a must in your pantry. Anchovies are small fish that are usually salted and canned in either brine or olive oil. They work really well as a salty seasoning and combine brilliantly with lamb and tomatoes. Capers are small berries that can be bought salted or in brine. I personally prefer the salted ones. They are smaller, with a lovely intense flavor. They work well in pasta sauces and stews and they're a great way to perk up a quick vegetable stir-fry. Make sure you rinse the salt off before using.

Beans and lentils

Cooked beans such as kidney or cannellini beans are an important staple in any pantry. Canned beans are brilliant for making dishes go further and adding essential protein to many vegetarian dishes. As canned beans are already cooked, they are less time-consuming to use than dried beans. Lentils work perfectly with fatty meats such as pork and lamb.

Honey

Honey is a great way to sweeten dishes and works well as part of a marinade and tenderizer. Keep a good-quality honey on hand and, if possible, one that is as local to you as possible.

BUYING MEAT
Chicken

It's really worth spending money on chicken. The more you spend, the better it is. Look for an organic or free-range bird. A frozen supermarket bird, battery-raised and fed on fishmeal until the moment of slaughter, has little chance of tasting good. Organic birds will look scrawnier than the plump-breasted, water-injected, oven-ready bird, but the flavor will be far superior.

BUYING FISH

If you can, find a local fishmonger with whom you can build a relationship and who will guide you to the freshest catch of the day. When buying fish, don't be afraid to ask where it comes from and how fresh it is. As well as asking, hold the fish and make sure that:
- The eyes are bright and shiny
- The flesh feels firm and is slippery and slimy
- The gills are bright
- The flesh resists pressure from your finger
- It has a clean smell, with no hint of ammonia

BUYING FRUITS AND VEGETABLES
Choosing vegetables

Fruits, vegetables and herbs are best bought, cooked and eaten when they are in season. They will be at their best for eating and will also be cheaper.

Try to buy local produce if you can. Most fruits and vegetables out of season have traveled a lot of "food miles." Even if you buy local produce, avoid vegetables and fruit that have been grown under cover out of season. They can use a lot of energy and cost a premium to produce.

The next important thing about buying vegetables is to make sure they are fresh. Vegetables don't have to look perfect or unblemished, as you will find when you buy organic, but they should be firm to the touch and heavy for their size.

Choosing fruit

Choose fruit that is heavy for its size. It should have a good fragrance, but if it smells too strong, it may be over-ripe.

If you are buying fruit that is not going to be eaten on the same day, buy it slightly unripe and ripen it at home.

Don't prepare fruit until you're ready to use it. Hulled strawberries do not last as long as unhulled, for example, because they can discolor and lose their flavor. If you cannot use the fruit, freeze it and use for dishes such as purées and ice creams.

Tips for the perfect stir-fry

As I have already mentioned, you don't need to spend a lot of money on a wok to get good results. A cheap one may last you just as long as an expensive, non-stick one. However, there are some simple ways that you can make your wok work for you.

Seasoning your wok

Put your wok on a low heat. Add 2 Tbsp of cooking oil and rub it over the inside of the wok using a paper towel. Make sure the whole surface is lightly coated with oil. Heat the wok slowly for about 15 minutes and then wipe it thoroughly with more paper towel. Repeat the process until the paper towel wipes clean.

Cleaning your work

To clean your wok, wash it in water without detergent. Dry it thoroughly, preferably by putting it over a low heat for a few minutes; this will prevent rusting. If it does rust, wash the wok with a gentle detergent and repeat the seasoning process.

Cooking

The most important thing when stir-frying is to have all your ingredients prepared ahead of time. Stir-frying is a very quick method of cooking and needs your total attention.

If you are not following a recipe, cut all the ingredients into bite-size pieces. Remember that certain vegetables take longer to cook than others. Vegetables with a high water content such as bok choy and peas will cook a lot quicker than denser vegetables such as carrots and broccoli.

Make sure your vegetables are washed and dry before cooking. This will keep them from boiling rather than frying. If they are too dry, try adding a few drops of water while stir-frying.

If you are using a cast-iron work, heat the wok or pan before adding any oil as this will heat the oil more quickly. However, if you have a non-stick pan or wok, do not heat it first as this may damage the lining of the pan. Drizzle the oil in the pan and coat it evenly. The oil will heat quicker this way. As a rule, always stir-fry over a high heat unless otherwise specified in the recipe. If the oil isn't hot enough, your ingredients will absorb the fat and end up soggy rather than crisp. If you are heating your wok to a high heat, never use cold-pressed or nut oils. Use a good peanut oil or vegetable oil instead. These heat to a much higher temperature and will not burn. Before adding other ingredients, season the oil by cooking a few pieces of garlic and ginger. (You may want to reduce the heat at this point to prevent burning.)

Stir the food constantly using a wooden spatula to make sure all the food is cooked evenly. Food falls down the side to the hottest part of the wok in the center, so keep everything moving.

Don't over-fill your wok or pan. This will reduce the temperature and make the ingredients boil instead of fry. If you're cooking for a larger group of people, stir-fry in batches, then return everything to the pan to quickly heat through.

Meat is normally stir-fried on high heat to seal in the juices. When stir-frying meat, wait a few seconds before tossing so that it has a chance to brown. Remove the meat from the wok when it changes color. At this point the meat is 80 percent cooked.

If the recipe calls for meat and vegetables, cook the meat first (see above) and then set it aside. When stir-frying vegetables, begin moving them immediately. Return the meat to the pan when the vegetables are almost cooked. This ensures that the meat is not overcooked, and that the meat and vegetables retain their individual flavors.

When adding sauce to vegetables and/or meat, form a "well" in the middle by pushing the ingredients up the sides of the wok. Add the sauce in the middle and stir to thicken before combining with the other ingredients.

Once the dish is cooked and complete, taste and adjust your seasonings as required. Enjoy!

Classics

If your only experience of chicken chow mein, Thai green chicken curry or sweet and sour pork is from your local takeout, now is the time to get out your wok. You can try all your favorite Chinese and Asian recipes at home and experience the real pleasure of each of these wonderful dishes.

The stir-fries in this chapter are all based on traditional and well-known dishes that you might find on a restaurant or takeout menu. The beauty of these recipes is that you can make your own delicious Asian food incredibly quickly, using fresh and tasty ingredients. All are easy to prepare, getting maximum results from minimum effort. Once you've stocked up your pantry with a few basic essentials you'll never need that takeout menu again!

Ingredients are easy to come by and can be found in most larger supermarkets. Otherwise, for an amazing variety of authentic ingredients, try and find a large Asian supermarket or shop around for a good mail order company that will deliver.

Thai green chicken curry

Thai green chicken curry

Perennial favorite

This fragrant curry is a favorite in Thai cooking. It can also be made with fish, seafood and vegetables.

Serves 4

2 Tbsp **peanut oil**
3 Tbsp **Thai green curry paste**
4 **skinless, boneless chicken thighs,** cut into bite-size chunks
14fl oz (400ml) **coconut cream**
1 Tbsp **brown sugar**
6 **small carrots,** peeled
4 **zucchini,** sliced
6 spears **purple sprouting broccoli,** trimmed
1 Tbsp **fish sauce (*nam pla*)**
2 **kaffir lime leaves,** torn, **or** grated rind of 1 lime
2 Tbsp **cilantro,** chopped **or**
   2 Tbsp **Thai basil leaves,** chopped to garnish

To serve:
Thai fragrant rice

Heat a large wok or frying pan and add the oil. Add 1 Tbsp green Thai curry paste and stir-fry for 1 minute. Add the chicken and stir-fry for a further 5 minutes until cooked. Remove and set aside.

Clean out the wok, add the coconut cream and bring to a boil over a low heat. Add the remaining green curry paste, stir for 1 minute, then add the brown sugar. Bring to a simmer and add the vegetables. Cook for 3–5 minutes until the vegetables are just cooked. Return the chicken to the pan and heat through for 2 minutes. Add the fish sauce and lime leaves, and mix everything together.

Garnish with cilantro or Thai basil leaves. Serve with Thai fragrant rice.

■ *If you want to make your own green curry paste, put the following ingredients in a food processor and blend until smooth: 2 fresh green chillies; 1 small onion, finely diced; 1 tsp ground coriander; the grated rind and juice of 1 lime; 1 lemongrass stalk; 1 garlic clove; 1 Tbsp soy sauce; 1 tsp ground cumin; 6 Tbsp chopped cilantro, 1 Tbsp grated fresh ginger and 2 Tbsp peanut oil.*

Lemon chicken

Hong Kong classic

This Hong Kong specialty usually consists of batter-coated chicken served with a sweet lemon sauce. This recipe is a healthier version that uses less sugar and omits the batter.

Serves 4

1lb (450g) **skinless, boneless chicken breasts,** cut into strips
1 **egg white,** lightly whisked
2 tsp **cornstarch**
4 Tbsp **peanut oil**

For the sauce:
½ cup (100ml) **chicken stock**
3 Tbsp **fresh lemon juice**
1 Tbsp **extra-fine sugar**
1 Tbsp **soy sauce**
1 Tbsp **rice wine**
2 **garlic cloves,** finely chopped
1 tsp **sesame oil**
2 **green onions,** finely sliced to garnish

To serve:
Steamed rice
Steamed green vegetables

Put the chicken strips in a bowl and combine with the egg white, cornstarch and 2 Tbsp oil. Cover and refrigerate for 10 minutes.

Heat a large frying pan or wok and add the remaining oil. Add the chicken strips and stir-fry for 5 minutes. Drain the chicken and set aside.

Wipe the wok clean and heat again until very hot. Add all the sauce ingredients except for the sesame oil and green onions. Bring to a boil over a high heat for 1 minute.

Return the chicken strips to the wok and stir-fry for 2 minutes until all the chicken is coated with the lemon sauce and heated through. Sprinkle over the sesame oil, garnish with green onions and serve with steamed rice and green vegetables.

Stir-fried beef with oyster sauce

Timeless

Originally, as the name suggests, oyster sauce was made from oysters, water and salt. However, it now contains cornstarch and caramel and has no fishy taste. It is cooked until concentrated and works well with red meats.

Serves 2–3

2 Tbsp **light soy sauce**
1 Tbsp **sesame oil**
2 Tbsp **rice wine or dry sherry**
1lb (450g) **sirloin or fillet steak,** cut into strips
2 Tbsp **peanut oil**
2 **garlic cloves,** finely sliced
1-in (2-cm) piece **fresh ginger,** peeled and grated
4 Tbsp **oyster sauce**
2 **green onions,** finely sliced to garnish

To serve:
Long-grain rice

In a small bowl, mix the soy sauce, sesame oil and rice wine or sherry. Add the beef and set aside to marinate for 10 minutes.

Heat a large frying pan or wok and add the peanut oil. Add the beef strips, garlic and ginger, and stir-fry for 2 minutes until seared but still pink inside. Remove the meat from the wok and drain off the oil.

Wipe the wok clean and re-heat over a high heat. Add the oyster sauce and bring to a simmer. Return the beef slices to the pan and toss them in the oyster sauce. Turn onto a plate, garnish with the green onions and serve with long-grain rice.

■ *Depending on the size of your wok, you may find it easier to stir-fry the beef in batches.*

Chicken chow mein

Chicken chow mein

Ever-popular

"Chow mein" means stir-fried noodles, and this must be one of the most popular Chinese takeout dishes of all time. It's versatile and a great dish for using up leftovers. You can add fish, meat, poultry or vegetables. It also makes a great salad served cold.

Serves 4

8oz (225g) **dried egg noodles**
2 Tbsp **sesame oil**
2 Tbsp **peanut oil**
3 or 4 **boneless chicken breasts,** cut into strips
2 **garlic cloves,** finely chopped
½ cup (50g) **snow peas**
2oz (50g) **cooked ham**
3 Tbsp **soy sauce**
1 Tbsp **rice wine or dry sherry**
3 **green onions,** finely chopped
1 Tbsp **sesame seeds,** toasted

Cook the noodles in a large pan of slightly seasoned boiling water for about 5–7 minutes until tender. Drain and sprinkle with 1 Tbsp of the sesame oil.

Meanwhile, heat a large frying pan or wok. When hot add 1 Tbsp of the peanut oil. Add the sliced chicken and stir-fry for about 2 minutes. Remove the chicken and set aside.

Re-heat the wok and add the remaining peanut oil. Add the garlic and stir-fry for 30 seconds. Add the snow peas and ham and stir-fry for a further 1 minute. Add the cooked noodles, soy sauce, rice wine or sherry, and green onions. Return the chicken and any juices to the pan and stir-fry for about 3–4 minutes or until heated through.

Add the remaining sesame oil, sprinkle with sesame seeds and give a final stir. Serve immediately.

Spicy Szechwan-style shrimp

Moreish

This is a fragrant sauce from the western province of Szechwan in China. It has now become a popular dish on any Chinese restaurant menu. It is incredibly versatile and works well with fish, chicken and red meats.

Serves 3–4

For the sauce:
1 Tbsp **hoisin sauce**
1 Tbsp **black bean sauce**
2 Tbsp **plum sauce**
1 Tbsp **dry sherry**
1 tsp **chilli paste**
1 Tbsp **soy sauce**
1 Tbsp **peanut oil**

1 Tbsp **peanut oil**
1-in (2.5-cm) **piece fresh ginger,** peeled and grated
1 **garlic clove,** finely chopped
3 **green onions,** finely sliced
1 lb (450g) **raw shrimp,** deveined with the tails left on
1 small bunch **cilantro,** to garnish

Combine all the sauce ingredients in a bowl and set aside.

Heat a large frying pan or wok over a high heat. Add the peanut oil and when it is very hot add the ginger, garlic and green onions. Stir-fry for 20 seconds and then add the shrimp. Stir-fry the shrimp for about 1 minute.

Add all the sauce ingredients from the bowl and continue to stir-fry for a further 2–3 minutes over a high heat. Serve at once, garnished with cilantro.

■ *If you can't find raw shrimp, use cooked and reduce the cooking time.*

Sweet and sour pork

Ever-popular

There are many versions of this popular Chinese classic. The most famous is minced pork dumplings, coated in a batter and deep-fried. This is a much simpler version.

Serves 2

2 Tbsp **peanut oil**
2 **garlic cloves**, finely sliced
1-in (2.5-cm) piece **fresh ginger**, peeled and grated
2 **green onions**, finely sliced
5½oz (155g) **pork tenderloin**, cut into thin slices
2 **red peppers**, deseeded and thinly sliced

For the sweet and sour sauce:
⅔ cup (150ml) **chicken stock**
2 Tbsp **rice wine or dry sherry**
3 Tbsp **soy sauce**
1 Tbsp **tomato paste**
3 Tbsp **rice vinegar**
1 Tbsp **sugar**

To serve:
Long-grain rice

Heat a frying pan or large wok over a high heat. Add the oil and when it is very hot and slightly smoking add the garlic, ginger and green onions. Stir-fry for 20 seconds.

Add the pork and stir-fry for 2 minutes. Add the red pepper and stir-fry for a further 1 minute.

Mix all the sauce ingredients together in a bowl until well blended. Pour over pork and vegetables and bring to a boil and simmer for 3 minutes. Serve immediately with long-grain rice.

Pad Thai

Thai classic

This is a classic Thai dish, perfect for using up any leftover chicken. Simply shred the chicken and add it in with the shrimp.

Serves 2–3

4oz (125g) rice noodles
Juice of 2 limes
½ tsp cayenne
2 tsp extra-fine sugar
2 Tbsp fish sauce (*nam pla*)
2 Tbsp peanut oil
9oz (250g) cooked tiger shrimp, peeled with tail shells left on
4 green onions, finely sliced
generous ½ cup (150g) bean sprouts
¼ cup (25g) salted peanuts, roughly chopped
1 small bunch cilantro
Lime zest, to garnish

To serve:
Lime quarters

Put the noodles in a large heatproof bowl, pour boiling water over them and leave for 4 minutes. Drain and refresh under cold running water.

Put the lime juice, cayenne, sugar and fish sauce in a bowl and mix well.

Heat a large frying pan or wok and add the oil. Stir-fry the shrimp for 2 minutes until browned and cooked through. Add the green onions and noodles, and combine well. Pour in the lime juice mixture and stir in the bean sprouts. Cook for 1 minute until everything is heated through. Sprinkle over the peanuts, cilantro and lime zest and serve with the lime quarters.

■ *Thai sweet chilli sauce makes a great accompaniment to this dish.*

Pad Thai

Meat feasts

Some recipes in this chapter are more familiar stir-fry dishes designed to be served with rice or noodles, but also introduced are new and imaginative ways to use your wok. There are versions of slow-cook classics such as Stir-fried beef chilli (page 44), spicy curries such as Very quick chicken curry (page 56) and dishes to serve with pasta including Spaghetti with pork, fennel and lemon (page 89).

With delicious stir-fry recipes using beef, chicken, duck, lamb and pork, there is a dish to suit every taste, whether you want to create something hot and spicy, or fresh and light.

Buying good meat is expensive, but worth it. That is where stir-frying comes into its own. If you've cooked a whole chicken or a lamb, pork or beef joint on the weekend, you can, with a well-stocked pantry, turn any leftover meat into magical meals in a matter of moments. If you stir-fry adding noodles and vegetables, a little meat goes a very long way.

Spicy beef stir-fry

Tangy

This is delicious served with rice or noodles, or over a baked potato topped with a dollop of sour cream.

Serves 4

2 Tbsp **soy sauce**
1 Tbsp **sesame oil**
1 tsp **cornstarch**
1lb (450g) **sirloin or fillet steak,** thinly sliced
2 Tbsp **peanut oil**
1 **mild red chilli,** finely diced
2 **garlic cloves,** finely chopped
2 Tbsp **fresh ginger,** finely chopped
1½ cups (225g) **fine green beans**
3 cups (225g) **brown-capped mushrooms,** sliced
1 **red pepper,** finely sliced
2 **small heads bok choy,** leaves separated from stem

To serve:
Fried rice or noodles

In a small bowl, combine the soy sauce, sesame oil and cornstarch, and marinate the steak for 10 minutes.

Heat a large wok or frying pan and add 1 Tbsp peanut oil. Add the chilli, garlic and ginger and stir-fry for 30 seconds. Add the beans, mushrooms and red pepper and stir-fry for a further 3–5 minutes until tender. Remove the vegetables and wipe the pan clean.

Re-heat the pan and add the remaining peanut oil. Stir-fry the beef strips in batches, for 2 minutes per batch. Remove and keep warm. Return the beef and vegetables to the pan. Add the bok choy and heat through. Serve with fried rice or noodles.

■ *If you like your meat well cooked, increase the cooking time by a minute or two.*

Spicy beef stir-fry

Beef with salsa verde

Italian

"Salsa verde" means green sauce in Italian. Classically served with red meat, it also works well with chicken and meaty white fish. The sauce can be made well in advance and stored in the fridge.

Serves 3–4

For the salsa verde:
1 small bunch **chopped flat-leaf parsley**
1 small bunch **mint leaves**
4 Tbsp **capers**, drained
12 **anchovy fillets in oil**, drained
2 **garlic cloves**
2 Tbsp **Dijon mustard**
Juice of 1 **lemon**
1 cup (220ml) **extra-virgin olive oil**

12oz (375g) **dried spaghetti**
2 Tbsp **peanut oil**
1lb (450g) **lean steak**, cut into strips
Freshly ground black pepper,
   to season

Put all the ingredients for the salsa verde into a processor or blender and process until smooth. Alternatively, pound by hand using a pestle and mortar.

Cook the spaghetti in a large pan of lightly salted boiling water for 8–10 minutes until cooked, then drain.

Meanwhile, heat a large frying pan or wok and add the oil. Stir-fry the beef strips in batches, for 2 minutes per batch. When all the meat is cooked, set aside and keep warm.

Re-heat the pan and return the beef to the pan with the salsa verde and spaghetti. Stir-fry for 2 minutes until well combined and everything is heated through. Season with black pepper.

Beef with a creamy mustard sauce

Warming

This makes a great supper dish for a cold evening, served with a piping hot jacket potato and a glass of fruity red wine.

Serves 3–4

3 Tbsp **peanut oil**
½ stick (55g) **butter**
2 **large sirloin steaks,** cut into thin strips
1 cup (225g) **broccoli florets,** roughly chopped
1 **onion,** finely diced
2 **cloves garlic,** finely chopped
4 **tomatoes,** cut into quarters
1 **small glass white wine**
2 tsp **wholegrain mustard**
⅔ cup (150ml) **crème fraîche or sour cream**
Snipped chives, to garnish

Heat 1 Tbsp oil and half the butter in a large frying pan or wok. When the pan is hot and slightly smoking, stir-fry the beef strips in two batches, for 2 minutes per batch, adding 1 Tbsp oil and the remaining butter. Remove the beef and set aside.

Clean out the pan and add the remaining oil. Add the broccoli, onion, garlic and tomatoes and stir-fry for 2–3 minutes. Remove and set aside. Reheat the wok and add the wine and simmer for 3 minutes until it is almost completely reduced.

Return the meat and vegetables to the pan. Add the mustard and crème fraîche or sour cream, and heat through, stirring constantly. Season to taste and serve at once, garnished with chives.

Spicy beef with Persian rice

Spicy beef with Persian rice

Fragrant

My father is a great cook and my children love his pilau rice. Here is his version of this delicious rice dish.

Serves 3–4

For the beef:
2 Tbsp **peanut oil**
1lb (450g) **sirloin steak,** thinly sliced
1 tsp **mild harissa paste**
4 **green onions,** finely sliced

For the rice:
3 **cardamom pods,** crushed
1 **cinnamon stick,** shredded
2½ cups (225g) **cooked basmati rice**
⅔ cup (150ml) **vegetable stock**

1 small bunch **flat-leaf parsley,**
   finely chopped
1 small bunch **mint,** finely chopped
2 Tbsp **raisins**
2 Tbsp **flaked almonds**

To serve:
Plain yogurt
Spinach

In a small bowl combine 1 Tbsp oil, the beef and harissa paste. Heat a large frying pan or wok. When the pan is just smoking, add the beef and the harissa paste. Stir-fry for 1 minute then add the green onions and stir-fry for a further minute. Remove the beef and onions from the pan and set aside.

Re-heat the pan and add the remaining oil. Add the cardamom and cinnamon and fry for 1 minute. Add the rice together with the stock, beef and onions and stir for 2–4 minutes until well combined and cooked through. If the mixture is dry, add a little water. Stir in the flat-leaf parsley, fresh mint, raisins and flaked almonds. Serve with plain yogurt and spinach.

■ *Wash freshly cooked rice in a sieve under cold running water to separate the grains and remove excess starch.*

Stir-fried beef chilli

Easy version

This is a stir-fry adaptation of a classic beef chilli but, of course, much quicker than the original.

Serves 3–4

3 Tbsp **peanut oil**
1 lb (450g) **sirloin steak**, cut into strips
1 tsp **ground cumin**
1 tsp **coriander seeds**, crushed
1 **onion**, peeled and finely chopped
2 **red peppers**, deseeded and finely sliced
2 **garlic cloves**, peeled and crushed
½ tsp **dried oregano**
1¾ cups (400g) **canned kidney beans**
½–1 tsp **chilli powder**
1 cup (200g) **canned tomatoes**
1 Tbsp **tomato paste**
1 small bunch **cilantro**, chopped

To serve:
Tortillas
2 **avocados**, peeled, pit removed and roughly chopped
Juice of 1 **lime**
Crème fraîche or sour cream

Heat a large frying pan or wok and add 1 Tbsp peanut oil. When the wok is hot and lightly smoking, add the beef, cumin and coriander seeds and stir-fry for 1 minute until browned. Remove and set aside. If necessary, cook in batches and set aside.

Clean out your wok or frying pan and add the remaining oil. Add the onion and red peppers and cook for 5 minutes over a medium heat until the onion is translucent, then add the garlic and cook for a further 1 minute. Add the oregano, kidney beans, chilli powder, tomatoes and tomato paste. Bring to a boil and simmer for 15 minutes.

Return the beef to the pan and continue cooking for a further 2 minutes until the beef is heated through. Scatter over the fresh cilantro and serve with soft tortillas, avocado, lime juice and crème fraîche or sour cream.

Steak and mushroom goulash

Hearty

This is a stir-fry version of the Hungarian slow-cooked goulash. The traditional version calls for sour cream but I've used plain yogurt to give a lower-fat result.

Serves 3–4

2 Tbsp **peanut oil**
1lb (450g) **sirloin steak,** trimmed and cut into strips
3 cups (225g) **brown-capped mushrooms,** cut into quarters
1 Tbsp **paprika**
8oz (250g) **passata**
4 Tbsp **vegetable stock**
⅔ cup (140g) **plain yogurt**
4 Tbsp **flat-leaf parsley,** chopped

To serve:
Flat noodles

Heat the oil in a large frying pan or wok and stir-fry the steak in batches. Remove and set aside.

Stir-fry the mushrooms for 3 minutes then add the paprika. Stir-fry for a further 2 minutes then add the passata and stock.

Bring to a boil and simmer for 10 minutes. Return the beef to the pan and simmer for a further 2 minutes until the beef is heated through. Stir through the yogurt, scatter over the flat-leaf parsley and serve with rice.

Warm Thai beef salad
Tender

The availability of salad leaves has improved dramatically over the last couple of years. An assortment of strong-tasting, peppery leaves such as arugula, mizuna and Tatsoi enhance the flavors of this dish.

Serves 3–4

1lb (450g) **beef fillet or sirloin steak**
3½oz (100g) **thin cellophane noodles**
1 **small cucumber,** peeled and diced
5oz (125g) **assorted salad leaves**
4 **green onions, sliced**
¼ cup (50g) **bean sprouts**

For the dressing:
2 Tbsp **fish sauce** (*nam pla*)
2 Tbsp **lime juice**
1 Tbsp **soy sauce**
1 tsp **peanut oil**
1 **red chilli,** deseeded and finely sliced
2 tsp **light brown sugar**

Heat the oil in a frying pan or large wok and stir-fry the beef in batches, for 2 minutes per batch. Remove and set aside.

Put the noodles in a heatproof bowl and cover with boiling water. Let stand for 7 minutes. Drain and set aside.

Place all the ingredients for the dressing in an airtight container and shake to combine.

To serve, combine the cucumber, salad leaves, green onions and bean sprouts in a large bowl. Stir in the noodles and beef, pour over the dressing and mix gently. Season to taste and serve immediately.

Warm Thai beef salad

Coriander chicken with satay sauce

Quick

I used to spend hours shelling peanuts for this recipe only to discover that peanut butter works just as well. This satay sauce is a great pantry dish and works brilliantly with tofu in place of the chicken.

Serves 4

4 skinless, boneless chicken
   breasts, thinly sliced
1 tsp coriander seeds, crushed
1 Tbsp honey
2 Tbsp vegetable oil

For the satay sauce:
2 Tbsp brown sugar
2 Tbsp curry paste
2 Tbsp peanut butter
1¾ cups (400g) canned coconut milk
Fresh cilantro, to garnish

To serve:
Long-grain rice
Bok choy

In a large bowl, mix the chicken pieces with the coriander seeds, honey and 1 Tbsp vegetable oil. Set aside to marinate for 10 minutes.

Meanwhile, make the satay sauce. Put the sugar, curry paste, peanut butter and coconut milk in a large frying pan or wok, bring to a boil and simmer for 2 minutes. Pour into a dish and set aside.

In the same wok, add the remaining oil, drain the chicken from the marinade and stir-fry for 5–7 minutes until the chicken is cooked. Pour over the satay sauce and heat through for 1 minute. Scatter over the cilantro and serve with rice and bok choy.

■ *The satay sauce solidifies as it cools. To thin the sauce, just return it to the pan and add 1–2 Tbsp water, then reheat.*

Cardamom-flavored chicken

Aromatic

Cardamom is a wonderful fragrant spice and is used in both sweet and savory dishes. For full flavor, crush the pods to release the tiny seeds. Cardomom is quite expensive, but you will find a little goes a long way in this recipe. It is thought to be an effective breath freshener, helping to eradicate garlic and alcohol smells on the breath.

Serves 3–4

2 Tbsp **peanut oil**
2 **garlic cloves,** finely chopped
6 **cardamom pods,** crushed
2 tsp **ground coriander**
2 **fresh chillies,** deseeded and finely chopped
4 **skinless chicken breasts,** cut into small cubes
⅔ cup (150ml) **coconut milk**
4 Tbsp **fresh cilantro**

To serve:
Basmati rice

Heat a large frying pan or wok and add the oil. Add the garlic, cardamom, coriander and chilli. Stir-fry for 30 seconds. Add the chicken and stir-fry for 5–8 minutes or until cooked through.

Stir in the coconut milk, bring to a boil and simmer. Scatter over the cilantro before serving.

Lemon chicken stir-fry with cashew nuts

Lemon chicken stir-fry with cashew nuts

Simple

Purple sprouting broccoli, often called poor man's asparagus, works perfectly as a substitute for zucchini in this recipe, as the stems are extremely tender. Alternatively you can also use the more common calabrese broccoli.

Serves 2–3

For the sauce:
⅔ cup (150ml) **fresh chicken stock**
1 tsp **cornstarch**
1 Tbsp **honey**
2 Tbsp **soy sauce**

2 Tbsp **peanut oil**
12oz (340g) **chicken fillets,** cut into strips
2 **garlic cloves,** finely sliced
2 large **zucchini,** thinly sliced
Grated rind of ½ **lemon and juice** of 1 **lemon**
½ cup (55g) **unsalted cashew nuts**

To serve:
Steamed brown rice

To make the sauce, mix the stock, cornstarch, honey and soy sauce in a small bowl and set aside.

Heat the oil in a large frying pan or wok. Add the chicken and stir-fry for 3–4 minutes until golden. Add the garlic and cook for a further minute. Remove from the pan and set aside.

Re-heat the pan and add 4 Tbsp water. When the water is boiling, add the zucchini and stir-fry for 2 minutes. Return the chicken to the pan with the sauce and cook for a further 2 minutes until the sauce has reduced.

Add the lemon rind, juice and cashew nuts; stir through until well combined and serve with steamed brown rice.

Chicken with raisins and toasted pine nuts

Exotic

The combination of fruit and nuts is popular in many food cultures. In North Africa they are added to fragrant couscous dishes. This is an adaptation of an old Persian dish and is perfect served with basmati rice.

Serves 3–4

2 Tbsp **sunflower oil**
1 **onion,** finely sliced
2 **garlic cloves,** finely chopped
1 **red chilli,** deseeded and finely
   sliced
1 tsp **garam masala**
1 tsp **ground turmeric**
1lb (450g) **cooked chicken,** shredded
2 Tbsp **pine nuts**
2 Tbsp **raisins**
1 small bunch **mint,** roughly chopped

To serve:
Lime wedges
Plain yogurt
Toasted pita bread

Heat a large frying pan or wok and add the oil. Stir-fry the onions for 5 minutes until golden. Add the garlic, chilli, garam masala and turmeric and cook for a further 1 minute.

Add the chicken, pine nuts and raisins, and stir-fry for 2 minutes until the chicken is heated through. Sprinkle over the mint and serve with wedges of lime, plain yogurt and toasted pita bread.

■ *This is a perfect dish for leftover chicken. For a more substantial meal, add cooked basmati rice.*

Balsamic chicken

Intense

Balsamic vinegar is a dark brown, syrupy vinegar with a smooth sweet flavor, produced in the Modena region of Italy. It is made from reduced grape juice that is then aged in wooden casts. Balsamic vinegar can be very expensive but the flavor is exceptional. Commercial balsamic vinegar is cheaper but not as intense in flavor. It's great in dressings and works well as a marinade or sprinkled over meat dishes

---

Serves 4

2 Tbsp **peanut oil**
4 **skinless, boneless chicken breasts,** sliced
2 **red onions,** peeled and sliced
4 **zucchini,** cut into strips
2 **garlic cloves,** thinly sliced
4 Tbsp **balsamic vinegar**
5oz (140g) **mozzarella,** roughly chopped
Salt and freshly ground black pepper, to season

To serve:
Roasted new potatoes
Seasonal salad

Heat a large frying pan or wok and add 1 Tbsp oil. When the pan is hot and slightly smoking, add the chicken slices. Stir-fry in batches for 5 minutes. Remove from the wok and keep warm.

Re-heat the pan and add the remaining oil. Add the onions and zucchini and stir-fry for 5 minutes. Add the garlic and continue to stir-fry for 1 minute. Pour in the balsamic vinegar and stir-fry for 2 minutes until the vinegar has reduced by half. Return the chicken to the pan and add the mozzarella. Stir well until the cheese begins to melt and the chicken is heated through. Season with salt and pepper and serve with roasted new potatoes and a seasonal salad.

Chicken, pea, mint and bacon pasta

Easy

If you can't find fresh peas, frozen peas work just as well. They are much better than canned ones, which usually have a higher salt content. Frozen peas are frozen at the time of picking so you can't get much fresher than that.

Serves 4

13oz (370g) **dried penne pasta**
1 tsp **olive oil**
2 Tbsp **peanut oil**
4 **skinless, boneless chicken breasts,** cut into strips
2 **garlic cloves,** peeled and finely chopped
8 strips **bacon,** roughly chopped
2½ cups (340g) **frozen peas,** cooked and drained
5oz (150g) **crème fraîche or sour cream**
1 large bunch **mint,** roughly chopped
4oz (110g) **mature Cheddar cheese,** grated

To serve:
Green salad

Heat a large pan of lightly salted water. When boiling, add the pasta and cook for 8–10 minutes. Drain and stir in a little olive oil.

Meanwhile, in a large frying pan or wok, heat the peanut oil and add the chicken slices. Stir-fry continuously for 3 minutes, then add the garlic and bacon and cook for a further 5 minutes. Add the peas, cooked pasta and crème fraîche or sour cream and stir-fry for a further 5 minutes. Stir in the mint and Cheddar. Serve with a fresh green salad.

■ *To save on the washing up, you can add the frozen peas to the pan in which you are cooking the pasta 5 minutes before the end of the pasta cooking time.*

Chicken with thyme, goat's cheese and tomatoes

Robust

Try to find a soft goat's cheese for this recipe. Thyme works perfectly with goat's cheese and, if you leave out the chicken, this recipe is great for vegetarians. Use fresh thyme rather than dried.

Serves 3–4

2 Tbsp **peanut oil**
4 **skinless, boneless chicken breasts,** cut into chunks
2 Tbsp **balsamic vinegar**
2 **garlic cloves,** finely chopped
1 Tbsp **fresh thyme,** chopped
1lb (450g) **vine or plum tomatoes,** cut into quarters
8oz (225g) **goat's cheese,** crumbled
Salt and freshly ground black pepper, to season
2 Tbsp **extra-virgin olive oil**

To serve:
Green salad
Oven-roasted new potatoes

Heat a large frying pan or wok and add 1 Tbsp of the oil. Add the chicken and stir-fry for 5 minutes until golden. Add the balsamic vinegar and continue to stir-fry for 2 minutes until the chicken is golden and cooked. If the pan gets too dry add 1–2 Tbsp water. Remove the chicken from the pan and set aside.

Re-heat the pan and add the remaining oil. Add the garlic and continue to stir-fry for 20 seconds. Add the thyme and tomatoes and cook for a further 2 minutes.

Return the chicken to the pan, heat through and add the goat's cheese. Season with salt and freshly ground black pepper, drizzle with olive oil and serve with a green salad and oven-roasted new potatoes.

Very quick chicken curry
Creamy

Adding fruit, nuts and yogurt transforms a simple dish into something special.

Serves 3–4

4 skinless, boneless chicken breasts, cut into strips
Juice of 1 lemon
4 Tbsp tikka or mild curry paste
2 Tbsp peanut oil
1 mango, peeled and sliced
2 garlic cloves, crushed
⅔ cup (150g) plain yogurt
scant ½ cup (55g) flaked almonds, toasted
4 Tbsp cilantro, roughly chopped

To serve:
Basmati rice

Put the chicken strips in a large bowl and sprinkle with lemon juice. Add the tikka or curry paste. Mix well. Set aside to marinate for 10 minutes.

Heat a large wok or frying pan and add 1 Tbsp oil. Add the chicken with its marinade and cook for 5–7 minutes until the chicken is golden and cooked. Remove and set aside.

Bring the wok back up to heat. Add the remaining oil, then the mango and garlic, and stir-fry for a further 1 minute. Return the chicken to the pan and stir-fry until the chicken is heated through. Stir in the yogurt. Sprinkle over the toasted almonds and cilantro and serve with basmati rice.

■ *If you want a curry with more of a kick, use a madras curry paste instead of tikka.*

Very quick chicken curry

Chicken with tarragon, leeks and crème fraîche

Elegant

Tarragon and chicken are a classic example of two ingredients that complement each other perfectly. When using tarragon in dishes such as this, it is best to add it at the end of cooking, as heat tends to decrease its flavor.

Serves 3–4

2 Tbsp **peanut oil**
4 **skinless, boneless chicken breasts,** sliced
1 **onion,** finely chopped
2 **garlic cloves,** roughly chopped
1lb (450g) **leeks,** finely sliced
scant 2 cups (425ml) **dry white wine**
1 Tbsp **Dijon mustard**
2 Tbsp **crème fraîche or sour cream**
1 Tbsp **fresh tarragon,** chopped
Salt and freshly ground black pepper, to season

To serve:
Mashed potatoes

Heat a large frying pan or wok and add the oil. When hot and almost smoking, add the chicken in batches and stir-fry for 4–5 minutes per batch until cooked and golden. Remove and drain on paper towel.

Re-heat the pan and add the onions, garlic and leeks, and stir-fry for 5 minutes until the onions and leeks are soft and golden. Pour in the white wine and cook for 2 minutes until the wine has reduced by three-quarters. Add the mustard and crème fraîche or sour cream and cook for 2 minutes, stirring continuously.

Stir in the chopped tarragon and season with salt and freshly ground black pepper. Serve with mashed potatoes.

■ *This makes a great pasta sauce and works well with short pasta such as penne or fusilli.*

Cajun chicken with beans and spinach

Flavorsome

Cajun spice mixes are readily available from shops and supermarkets. They do vary so it's good to experiment to find one you like. Basically the ingredients are salt with a mix of cayenne pepper, onion powder, garlic powder, thyme, basil and bay leaf.

Serves 3–4

2 Tbsp **peanut oil**
8 **skinless, boneless chicken thighs,** cut into thick strips
2 Tbsp **Cajun spice mix**
2 **red onions,** sliced
2 **garlic cloves,** finely chopped
1 **red chilli,** finely chopped
1¾ cups (400g) canned **navy beans,** drained
⅔ cup (150ml) **chicken or vegetable stock**
12oz (340g) **fresh spinach**
Juice of 1 **lime**

To serve:
Crusty garlic bread
Green salad

Heat 1 Tbsp of the oil in a large frying pan or wok until the pan is almost smoking. Add the chicken slices and Cajun spice mix and stir-fry for 5–8 minutes. If the pan gets dry, add a few tablespoons of water. When the chicken is cooked, remove and set aside.

Re-heat the pan and add the remaining oil. Stir-fry the onion, garlic and chilli for 5 minutes. Add the beans and stir to combine well with the onions. Add the stock, bring to a boil and simmer for 10 minutes. Return the chicken to the pan, add the spinach and stir through for 1 minute until it has wilted.

Drizzle over the lime juice and serve with crusty garlic bread and a green salad.

Moroccan lemon and green olive chicken stir-fry

Moroccan lemon and green olive chicken stir-fry

Fragrant

Traditionally, Moroccan cooking uses preserved lemons. They are soft and have a subtle flavor, and they are now readily available in supermarkets or ethnic shops. In this recipe the preserved lemons give a fresh flavor to this light stir-fry dish.

Serves 4

2 Tbsp **olive oil**
1 **red onion,** sliced
2 **garlic cloves,** finely chopped
1 small **cinnamon stick,** shredded
1lb (450g) **skinless, boneless chicken fillets,** sliced
1 **preserved lemon,** finely chopped
generous ½ cup (140g) **green olives,** pitted
⅔ cup (150ml) **chicken stock**
1 large handful **cilantro,** roughly chopped
generous 1 cup (110g) **flaked almonds,** toasted

To serve:
Couscous

Heat a large frying pan or wok and add 1 Tbsp of the oil. Add the onion and stir-fry for 5 minutes until golden. Add the garlic and cinnamon and continue to stir-fry for 1 minute. Remove and set aside.

Re-heat the wok and add the remaining oil. Stir-fry the chicken for 5–8 minutes until golden. If the pan gets too dry, add 1–2 Tbsp water or stock.

Scatter the lemon pieces and olives over the chicken. Pour over the stock and return the onions and garlic to the pan. Bring to a boil and simmer for 5 minutes. Sprinkle over the fresh cilantro and flaked almonds and serve with couscous.

■ *If you can't find preserved lemons, boil a lemon for 30 minutes in a small pan of water. Discard the flesh and cut the skin into strips.*

Greek spiced chicken with red wine and prunes
Robust

My cousin Lena often serves this slow-cook Greek stew with lamb. I've adapted the recipe to make a delicious stir-fry supper. Use chicken thighs as the flavor is much stronger than white meat and works well with the prunes.

Serves 4

2 Tbsp **peanut oil**
6 **skinless, boneless chicken thighs,** cut into strips
1 **large onion,** thinly sliced
2 **garlic cloves, sliced**
1¾ cups (400g) canned **chopped tomatoes**
4 **cloves**
1 small **cinnamon stick**
1 tsp **ground coriander**
1 small glass **red wine**
8 **prunes,** soaked in water to plump up, stones removed and cut in half
Chopped **mint,** to garnish

To serve:
Lemon potatoes (see tip)

Heat a large frying pan or wok and add 1 Tbsp oil. When the pan is hot and almost smoking, stir-fry the chicken for 5 minutes until browned. If the pan gets dry, add a little water to prevent the chicken from sticking. Remove the chicken and set aside.

Clean the wok, add the remaining oil, and stir-fry the onion for 10 minutes. Add the garlic and cook for a further 2 minutes. Add the remaining ingredients except for the mint, bring to a boil and simmer for 10 minutes. Return the chicken to the pan and cook for a further 5 minutes until the chicken is heated through. Sprinkle over the mint and serve with lemon potatoes.

■ *To make lemon potatoes, pre-heat the oven to 375°F (190°C). Slice 4 large potatoes and layer them in a buttered ovenproof dish. Season each layer with salt, freshly ground black pepper and a little lemon juice. Drizzle the top with olive oil, cover with foil and bake for 30–40 minutes.*

Spicy coconut chicken

Thai

Thai red curry paste is a versatile curry sauce that is a milder version of the Thai green curry paste. It works well as a marinade as well as a condiment.

Serves 3–4

2 Tbsp **peanut oil**
1lb (450g) **chicken thigh fillets,** cut into strips
2 **green onions,** thickly sliced
2 **red peppers,** deseeded and roughly chopped
1¾ cups (400ml) canned **coconut milk**
3 Tbsp **Thai red curry paste**
1 Tbsp **fish sauce** (*nam pla*)
Basil leaves, shredded, to garnish

To serve:
Thai fragrant rice

Heat the oil in a large frying pan or wok. Stir-fry the chicken in batches, for 5 minutes per batch, until browned and cooked. Remove from the pan and set aside.

Heat the remaining oil and stir-fry the green onions and pepper for 5 minutes until just soft. Return the chicken to the pan, then add the coconut milk, red curry paste and fish sauce. Stir and bring to a boil. Sprinkle the basil over and serve with Thai fragrant rice.

Spiced duck with honey and orange

Citrussy

Some partnerships are timeless, and duck and orange is no exception. The Chinese five-spice powder adds an interesting Asian twist to the beautiful crispy duck.

Serves 4

4 **duck breasts skin on,** cut into
   1-in (2.5-cm) strips
2 Tbsp **Chinese five-spice powder**
1 pinch **salt**
2 Tbsp **peanut oil**
2 **cloves**
1 **cinnamon stick**
Juice of 1 **orange**
1 Tbsp **honey**
1 **star anise**
2 Tbsp **soy sauce**
Green onion and cucumber,
   to garnish

To serve:
2¾ cups (250g) **cooked brown rice**
Plum sauce

Score the skin of the duck with a sharp knife and dust the strips all over with the five-spice powder and a pinch of salt.

Put the duck strips skin-side down in a cold wok or frying pan. Bring it slowly to a medium-low temperature so the white fat turns into wonderfully thick, crispy crackling. Cook for about 15 minutes. Turn the strips over and cook for a further 5 minutes. Remove the duck from the wok and set aside.

Heat the oil in the pan and add the cloves, cinnamon, orange juice, honey, star anise and soy sauce. Stir-fry for 2 minutes and return the duck to the pan to re-heat.

Garnish with the green onion and cucumber, and serve with brown rice and plum sauce.

Spiced duck with honey and orange

Duck breasts with blackberries

Fruity

Duck has a rich, fatty taste that works well with fruit sauces. If you can't find blackberries, replace with apples or pears.

Serves 4

2 Tbsp **peanut oil**
4 **duck breasts skin on,** cut into
    ½-in (1-cm) strips
2 **shallots,** peeled and finely chopped
1 **red chilli,** deseeded and finely
    chopped
1½ cups (340g) **blackberries**
¼ cup (55g) **extra-fine sugar**
Grated rind and juice of 1 **orange**
1 small glass **port or red wine**

Heat a large frying pan or wok, add the oil and heat until the pan is just beginning to smoke. Add the duck strips and stir-fry for 5 minutes until golden.

Add the shallots and cook for a further 2 minutes, making sure they don't burn. Add the chilli for 1 further minute and then the blackberries, sugar, orange rind and juice, and port. Bring to a boil and simmer for 10 minutes before serving.

Warm chicken and avocado salad

Impressive

A quick and easy summer salad served with a sweet honey dressing. For total indulgence, try adding crumbled feta cheese.

Serves 4

For the dressing:
¼ cup (60ml) **olive oil**
2 Tbsp **lemon juice**
1 tsp **honey**
1 tsp **mustard**
1 **garlic clove,** crushed

2 Tbsp **peanut oil**
4 **chicken breast fillets,** each cut into thin strips
6 strips **bacon,** roughly chopped
4 **green onions,** thickly sliced
½ cup (55g) **pecan nuts,** toasted
2 **medium avocados,** pitted, peeled and sliced
3¾ cups (170g) **mixed salad leaves**

In a small screw-top jar, combine the oil, lemon juice, honey, mustard and garlic, and shake well.

Heat a large frying pan or wok and add the oil. Stir-fry the chicken for 5–8 minutes until golden and cooked. If the chicken starts sticking to the pan, add 1–2 Tbsp water and continue to stir-fry. When the chicken is cooked, remove and set aside.

Re-heat the wok and stir-fry the bacon for 5 minutes until crisp. Return the chicken to the wok with the green onions and pecan nuts. Stir-fry for a further 2 minutes.

Tip the chicken and bacon into a large bowl and add the avocado and salad leaves. Drizzle with the dressing and serve.

■ *To prevent avocados from going brown, sprinkle with lemon juice.*

Lamb pilaf with apricots and almonds

Lamb pilaf with apricots and almonds

Exotic

Good-quality lamb can be very expensive, so this is a great recipe for leftovers. You can also substitute the lamb with chicken or beef if you wish.

Serves 3–4

2 Tbsp **peanut oil**
1 lb (450g) **lean lamb fillet,** cut into bite-size chunks
1 **large onion,** finely sliced
2 **garlic cloves,** finely sliced
2 tsp **ground cinnamon**
3¼ cups (250g) **basmati rice,** cooked
⅔ cup (150ml) **chicken or vegetable stock**
⅓ cup (55g) **dried apricots**
generous ½ cup (55g) **flaked almonds,** lightly toasted
1 large bunch **cilantro,** roughly chopped

To serve:
Plain yogurt
Lemon wedges
Naan bread

Heat a large frying pan or wok and when hot add 1 Tbsp oil. When the pan is smoking, add the lamb and stir-fry in batches, for 5 minutes per batch. Remove and drain on paper towel.

Clean out the pan and add the remaining oil. Add the onion and stir-fry for 5 minutes until golden. Add the garlic and cinnamon and stir-fry for a further 1 minute.

Return the lamb to the pan and add the rice, stock, apricots and toasted almonds. Stir through for 5 minutes until the rice is hot and the lamb is heated through. Sprinkle over the mint and serve with bowls of yogurt, lemon wedges and naan bread.

Lamb curry

Aromatic

Garam masala is a mix of spices common in Indian cuisine. It is usually added to curries at the end of cooking as a seasoning so the flavor is not lost. Its main ingredients are cinnamon, cloves and nutmeg, although there are many other slight variations. This is a great mixture to add to a marinade to add pungency.

Serves 4

For the marinade:
3 **garlic cloves**
2 tsp **fresh ginger, grated**
⅔ cup (150g) **plain yogurt, drained**
1 Tbsp **peanut oil**
2 Tbsp **garam masala**
1lb (450g) **lean lamb,** cut into
  bite-size chunks

For the curry:
2 Tbsp **peanut oil**
2 **red onions,** cut into wedges
5 cups (225g) **cherry tomatoes,**
  halved
1 tsp **ground cumin**
3 Tbsp **fresh cilantro,** chopped

To serve:
Plain yogurt
Mango chutney
Indian bread

To make the marinade, mash together the garlic and ginger in a blender and add the yogurt, oil and garam masala. Coat the lamb with the mixture and marinate for 30 minutes.

Heat a large frying pan or wok and add 1 Tbsp oil. When the oil begins to smoke, remove the lamb from the marinade and stir-fry in batches, for 5–7 minutes per batch. When all the lamb has been cooked, set aside and keep warm.

Wipe the pan and add the remaining oil. Add the red onion and stir-fry for 5 minutes until golden. Add the tomatoes and ground cumin, and stir-fry for a further 2 minutes until the tomatoes begin to break down.

Return the lamb to the pan and cook for 2 minutes to heat through. Sprinkle over the cilantro and serve with yogurt, mango chutney and Indian bread.

Lamb with tomatoes, green beans and oregano

Mediterranean

Unlike most herbs, oregano is at its best when dried. Although it is mainly used in Greek and Italian cooking, it also works surprisingly well with hot and spicy food.

Serves 4

2 Tbsp **peanut oil**
1lb (450g) **lean, boneless lamb,**
    cut into chunks
1¼ cups (225g) **green beans**
1 **sprig fresh thyme**
2 **red onions, sliced**
3 **garlic cloves,** finely chopped
1¾ cups (400g) canned **chopped**
    tomatoes
⅔ cup (150g) **black kalamata olives,**
    pitted
2 tsp **dried oregano**
1 tsp **wholegrain mustard**

To serve:
Pasta or rice

Heat a large frying pan or wok, add 1 Tbsp oil and stir-fry the lamb in batches, for 5 minutes per batch, until well seared. Remove from the pan and set aside.

Heat the remaining oil in the pan and add the beans, thyme and onions, and stir-fry for 3–4 minutes until the onions are golden. Add the garlic and continue stir-frying for 1 minute.

Add the tomatoes, olives and oregano and stir-fry for a further 5 minutes. Add the mustard, bring to a boil and simmer for 10 minutes. Serve with pasta or rice.

Harissa lamb with zucchini and chickpeas

Fiery

I first came across harissa at my local Moroccan restaurant and fell in love with it. There are many variations of this fiery condiment, both in heat and flavor. I prefer a milder harissa paste and often use it as a spicy rub for red meats.

Serves 3–4

1 Tbsp **mild harissa paste**
1lb (450g) **lean, boneless lamb,** cut into slices
2 Tbsp **peanut oil**
2 **garlic cloves,** finely sliced
8oz (225g) **zucchini,** thinly sliced
1¾ cups (400g) canned **cooked chickpeas**
Juice of 1 **lemon**
1 **small bunch flat-leaf parsley,** roughly chopped
1 **small bunch cilantro,** roughly chopped

To serve:
Couscous
Yogurt

Rub the harissa paste into the lamb and leave to marinate for 10 minutes.

Heat a large wok or frying pan and add 1 Tbsp oil. Add the lamb and stir-fry for 3 minutes until well seared but still pink. If you have to do this in batches, drain each batch on paper towel.

Wipe the wok and heat the remaining oil. Add the garlic and zucchini and stir-fry for 2 minutes, making sure the garlic does not burn. Add the chickpeas and lemon juice and return the lamb to the pan. Stir-fry for a further 2 minutes until heated through. Stir through the flat-leaf parsley and cilantro and serve with couscous and yogurt.

■ *If you don't like spicy food, omit the harissa paste altogether.*

Lamb with artichoke hearts, lemon and dill

Sophisticated

I always have a can of artichoke hearts in my pantry as they're incredibly versatile. For an unusual touch, serve them sliced in a bowl of steaming potatoes with butter or mint.

Serves 4

13oz (370g) **dried spaghetti**
Olive oil, for sprinkling
2 Tbsp **vegetable oil**
1lb (450g) **lamb,** cut into slices
2 **garlic cloves,** finely chopped
1¾ cups (400g) canned **artichoke hearts,** drained and finely sliced
1 small bunch **dill**
1 small bunch **mint**
Grated rind and juice of 1 **lemon**
4 Tbsp **Parmesan cheese,** grated
Extra-virgin olive oil, for drizzling

Heat a large pan of lightly salted water. When boiling, add the pasta and cook for 10 minutes. Drain and set aside.

Meanwhile, heat a large frying pan or wok and add the vegetable oil. When hot add the lamb and stir-fry for 5 minutes. Add the garlic and stir-fry for a further 1 minute. Add the artichoke hearts and cook for a further 2 minutes until heated through.

Stir in the dill, mint, lemon rind and lemon juice. Stir into the pasta and heat through. Scatter over the Parmesan and drizzle over a little extra-virgin olive oil.

Lamb with peppers, feta and olives

Rich

The sourness of the feta cuts perfectly through the richness of the lamb. Try and find a good, crumbly feta from Greece or Turkey rather than a processed variety. You might have to go to your local deli for the best choice.

Serves 4

1lb (450g) **lamb fillets,** sliced
2 Tbsp **olive oil**
Juice of 1 **lemon plus extra for**
  sprinkling
1 tsp **dried oregano**
1 Tbsp **peanut oil**
1 **red onion,** finely sliced
2 **red peppers** and 2 **green peppers,**
  deseeded and finely sliced
2 **garlic cloves,** crushed
¾ cup (170g) **black olives,** pitted
8oz (225g) **feta cheese**
1 small bunch **flat-leaf parsley,**
  roughly chopped

To serve:
Crusty bread
Green salad

Combine the lamb with the oil, lemon juice and oregano. Cover and refrigerate for 15 minutes.

Heat a large wok or frying pan, remove the lamb from the marinade and stir-fry for 5 minutes until the lamb is cooked and browned. You may have to cook the lamb in batches so drain on paper towel. When all the lamb is cooked, set aside and keep warm.

Heat the peanut oil in a large frying pan or wok. Add the onion and peppers and stir-fry for 5 minutes. Add the garlic and stir-fry for a further 2 minutes. Return the lamb to the pan with the olives and feta and stir-fry until hot. Sprinkle with flat-leaf parsley and a little more lemon juice. Serve with a green salad and crusty bread.

■ *The best olives to use for this dish are the Greek kalamata. They are black, oval-shaped and have a lovely bitter flavor.*

Lamb with peppers, feta and olives

Greek lamb

Spiced

Cinnamon gives this dish top billing. Like many ground spices, it loses its aroma and flavor quickly, so buy in small quantities and store in an airtight container.

Serves 4

2 Tbsp **peanut oil**
1lb (450g) **lean lamb fillet,** cut into thin slices
2 **onions,** cut into quarters
3 **green peppers,** deseeded and sliced
2 Tbsp **raisins**
3 **cloves**
2 tsp **coriander seeds, crushed**
2 tsp **cinnamon**
1 **small bunch flat-leaf parsley,** roughly chopped

To serve:
Hummus
Lemon wedges
Pita bread

Heat a large frying pan or wok and add 1 Tbsp oil. Add the lamb and stir-fry in batches, for 5 minutes per batch. When all the lamb is cooked, set aside and keep warm.

Re-heat the pan and add the remaining oil. Add the onions, green peppers, raisins, cloves, coriander seeds and cinnamon and stir-fry for 3–5 minutes.

Add the lamb to the vegetables and stir-fry for 2 minutes until all the ingredients are well combined and heated through.

Sprinkle with flat-leaf parsley and serve with hummus, lemon wedges and pita bread.

Classic French lamb

Quick-cook

This is an adaptation of the classic French bistro dish of lamb with flageolet beans. It is traditionally a slow-cooked dish but it's been recreated here as a quick-cook meal. If you've cooked roast lamb the day before, this is a great way to use up leftovers.

Serves 4

2 Tbsp **peanut oil**
1lb (450g) **lean, boneless lamb,** cut into cubes
1 large **red onion,** finely sliced
8 **cherry tomatoes**
2 **garlic cloves**
2 sprigs **rosemary**
1 small glass **white wine**
4 **anchovy fillets,** roughly chopped
1¾ cups (400g) canned **flageolet or navy beans**
4 Tbsp **passata**

To serve:
Creamy potatoes (see tip at right)

Heat a large frying pan or wok and add 1 Tbsp peanut oil. When the pan is hot and smoking, add the lamb.
Depending on the size of your wok, cook the lamb in batches. When all the lamb is cooked, remove and set aside.

Re-heat the pan or wok and add the remaining oil. Stir-fry the onions, tomatoes and garlic for 5 minutes. Add the rosemary, wine and anchovies, and continue cooking for 5 minutes until the wine has reduced by two-thirds.

Return the lamb to the wok and add the beans and passata. Bring to a boil and simmer for 10 minutes. Serve with creamy potatoes (see below).

■ *For a quick, creamy potato accompaniment, crush 3 hot, cooked floury potatoes with a little double cream and olive oil. Sprinkle over some Gruyère cheese and pop under the grill for 2 minutes until the cheese starts to melt.*

Quick stir-fry moussaka

Quick stir-fry moussaka

Ever-popular

Chargilled eggplants are available in most supermarkets and take a lot of work out of this dish. If you want to use a less fatty meat, replace the lamb with chicken or pork.

Serves 3–4

2 Tbsp **olive oil**
1lb (450g) **ground lamb**
1 **large onion,** finely chopped
2 **garlic cloves,** finely chopped
4 Tbsp **passata**
2 tsp **ground cinnamon**
2 tsp **dried mint**
1 cup (225g) **chargrilled eggplants in olive oil (from a jar)**
½ cup (100g) **chargrilled peppers (from a jar)**

To serve:
Plain yogurt, sprinkled with ground cinnamon
Green salad

Heat a large frying pan or wok and add 1 Tbsp oil. Add the ground lamb and cook over a high heat in batches, for 5 minutes per batch, breaking the meat up with a fork. This prevents it from cooking in large lumps. When all the meat is cooked, set it aside.

Re-heat the pan and add the remaining oil. Stir-fry the onions for 5 minutes, then add the garlic and stir-fry for a further 2 minutes.

Return the meat to the pan with the passata, cinnamon and dried mint. Bring to a boil and simmer for 10 minutes. Add the eggplants and peppers and cook for a further 5 minutes. Serve with plain yogurt, sprinkled with ground cinnamon, and a green salad.

■ *To make your own chargrilled eggplants, slice thinly and scatter over some salt. Allow the bitter juices to run out, then wash the eggplant and pat dry. Place on a baking tray and drizzle over some olive oil. Pop in a moderate oven for 20 minutes until cooked. Place in a non-metallic container and cover with olive oil. These will keep for 1 week in the fridge.*

Merguez sausages with beans

Filling

My friend Ray, a butcher, makes the most amazing Merguez sausages. They originate from Morocco and are made using ground lamb, cumin and harissa. If you can't get hold of the real thing, replace it with a spicy Italian sausage.

Serves 3–4

2 Tbsp **peanut oil**
4 **merguez sausages**, cut into chunks
1¾ cups (400g) canned **borlotti or cannellini beans**
1¾ cups (400g) canned **chopped tomatoes**
3½ cups (450g) **green beans**, cooked and drained
1 small bunch **flat-leaf parsley**

To serve:
Crusty bread or mashed potatoes

Heat a large wok or frying pan and add the oil. Stir-fry the sausages for 5 minutes until well seared.

Add the beans, tomatoes and green beans. Bring to a boil, then simmer for 10 minutes until heated through. Add the parsley and stir through. Serve with crusty bread or mashed potatoes.

Lamb with cumin and orange

Intense

I use cumin seeds a lot when I cook, especially with lamb. To get the best flavor always fry or toast the cumin first in a dry, non-stick pan or a hot oven. Make sure you buy the seeds in small quantities as it quickly loses its aroma.

Serves 3–4

2 Tbsp **peanut oil**
1lb (450g) **lamb fillet,** sliced
2 **garlic cloves,** crushed
1 tsp **cumin**
1½ cups (370g) **broccoli florets**
Grated rind and juice of 1 **orange**
Extra-virgin olive oil, for drizzling
Freshly ground black pepper, for
    seasoning

To serve:
Rice pilaf

Heat a large frying pan or wok and add the oil. When hot, add the lamb, garlic and cumin and stir-fry for 5 minutes. Depending on the size of your wok you may need to ccok the lamb in batches. Remove and keep warm.

Add the orange juice, orange rind and broccoli and stir-fry for 2 minutes. Return the lamb to the pan and heat through. Drizzle with olive oil and season with freshly ground black pepper. Serve with rice pilaf.

■ *For a garnish, sprinkle orange quarters with sugar, thyme and a little olive oil and bake in the oven for 15 minutes at 400°F (200°C).*

Pork with pineapple and chilli

Sweet and sour

This is a classic sweet and sour combination. I usually recommend using fresh fruit, but for this recipe canned pineapple work just as well.

Serves 2–3

For the marinade:
2 Tbsp **light soy sauce**
2 Tbsp **Shaoxing rice wine or dry sherry**
2 tsp **sesame oil**
1 tsp **cornstarch**
1lb (450g) **pork tenderloin,** cut into thin strips

2 Tbsp **peanut or vegetable oil**
2 **garlic cloves,** crushed
1 **red chilli,** deseeded and finely chopped
1 cup (225g) **fresh or canned pineapple chunks**
1 Tbsp **soy sauce**
2 tsp **sugar**
3 Tbsp **cilantro,** roughly chopped

To serve:
Stir-fried vegetables
Egg-fried rice

Combine the marinade ingredients in a medium-sized bowl. Add the pork and mix well. Marinate for 15 minutes.

Heat the oil in a large frying pan or wok. When very hot add the garlic and chilli and stir-fry for 15 seconds or until golden brown. Remove the pork from the marinade, add to the pan and stir-fry for 3 minutes.

Finally, add the pineapple, soy sauce and sugar and continue to stir-fry for 3 minutes. Sprinkle over the chopped cilantro and serve with stir-fried vegetables and rice.

Pork with pineapple and chilli

Pork with cider, apple and sage

Pork with cider, apple and sage

Classic re-take

This is an adaptation of the classic pork with applesauce. Not only is it quicker than the original but it's also a lot healthier as the fat content is considerably lower.

Serves 2–3

2 Tbsp **peanut or vegetable oil**
1lb (450g) **lean pork,** cut into ½-in (1-cm) slices
2 **apples,** cored and cut into wedges
2 **garlic cloves,** finely chopped
1 Tbsp **fresh sage,** chopped
4 Tbsp **crème fraîche or sour cream**
1 tsp **wholegrain mustard**
Salt and freshly ground black pepper, to season
Deep-fried sage leaves (optional)

To serve:
Seasonal greens
Mashed potatoes

Heat a large frying pan or wok and add the oil. When the pan is slightly smoking, add the pork in batches and stir-fry, for 5 minutes per batch, until all the pork is golden. Drain on paper towel. When all the pork is cooked, set aside.

Wipe the pan clean, heat it again, and add the remaining oil. Add the apples, garlic and sage and stir-fry for 2 minutes. Return the pork to the pan and stir-fry for 2 minutes until the pork is heated through. Place on a serving plate.

Return the wok to the heat and combine the crème fraîche or sour cream and mustard. Stir-fry for 30 seconds then pour over the pork and apples. Season with salt and freshly ground black pepper. Garnish with deep-fried sage leaves (if liked). Serve with seasonal greens and creamy mashed potatoes.

Stir-fried pork with leeks and mustard

Mild

Dijon mustard is a mild French mustard and works very well with leeks. If you can't find mustard seeds, use a wholegrain mustard instead. A strong English mustard would be too harsh with this dish.

Serves 2–3

2 Tbsp **peanut oil**
1lb (450g) **pork tenderloin,**
 cut into slices
1 Tbsp **mustard seeds**
4 **medium-sized leeks,**
 trimmed and thinly sliced
2 Tbsp **Dijon mustard**
2 Tbsp **cider vinegar**
4 Tbsp **crème fraîche or sour cream**

To serve:
Mashed potatoes

Heat a large frying pan or wok and add 1 Tbsp oil. When the oil begins to smoke add the pork tenderloin in batches and cook, for 5 minutes per batch. Drain on paper towel. When all the pork is cooked, set aside and wipe the pan.

Re-heat the pan and add the remaining oil. When the pan begins to smoke, add the mustard seeds and stir-fry for 10 seconds until they start popping. Add the leeks and stir-fry for a further 3 minutes until golden. Add the mustard and vinegar and stir for 2 minutes. Stir in the crème fraîche or sour cream. Return the pork to the pan and heat through for 2 minutes. Serve with creamy mashed potatoes.

Sesame pork with broccoli and mushrooms

Chinese

Shiitake mushrooms are Chinese mushrooms that have a very strong flavor and spongy texture. The Chinese call them fragrant, or delicious, mushrooms. For a firmer texture and a milder flavor, replace with chestnut or brown cap mushrooms.

Serves 3–4

⅔ cup (150ml) **chicken stock**
1 tsp **cornstarch**
1 Tbsp **soy sauce**
2 Tbsp **peanut oil**
1lb (450g) **pork tenderloin,** sliced
2 **garlic cloves,** finely chopped
4 **green onions,** finely sliced
scant 1 cup (200g) **broccoli florets,** roughly chopped
1½ cups (110g) **shiitake or chestnut mushrooms,** sliced
1 **red pepper,** deseeded and sliced
2 Tbsp **sesame seeds,** lightly toasted
Sesame oil, for drizzling

To serve:
Rice

Combine the chicken stock, cornstarch and soy sauce in a bowl. Blend well and set aside.

Heat a large frying pan or wok and add 1 Tbsp oil. Add the pork in batches and stir-fry for 5 minutes per batch, until the pork is well browned. When all the pork is cooked, set aside and keep warm.

Wipe the pan and add the remaining oil. Add the garlic and green onions and stir-fry for 1 minute until brown. Add the broccoli, mushrooms, pepper and the stock mixture to the pan. Bring to a boil and simmer for 5 minutes. Add the cooked pork and continue cooking for 2 minutes until the liquid has reduced and thickened.

Sprinkle over the toasted sesame seeds and drizzle over a little sesame oil. Serve with rice.

Spaghetti with pork, fennel and lemon

Citrussy

Fennel has a wonderful aniseed flavor and benefits from frying as it brings out the sweetness and makes it less tart.

Serves 4

14oz (375g) **dried spaghetti**
Olive oil, for sprinkling
2 Tbsp **peanut oil**
12oz (340g) **pork tenderloin,**
  sliced thinly
2 **fennel bulbs,** finely sliced
2 **garlic cloves,** finely sliced
1 small glass **white wine**
Grated zest and juice of 1 **lemon**
2 Tbsp **pine nuts,** lightly toasted
Grated Parmesan cheese, to serve
Extra-virgin olive oil, for drizzling

Heat a large pan of lightly salted water. When boiling, add the pasta and cook for 8 minutes. Drain and sprinkle with olive oil.

Meanwhile, heat a large frying pan or wok and add 1 Tbsp of the peanut oil. Stir-fry the pork in batches for 5 minutes per batch. Drain on paper towel. If the pan gets too dry, add 1–2 Tbsp extra water. When all the pork is cooked, set aside and wipe the pan.

Re-heat the pan and add the remaining oil. Add the fennel and garlic and stir-fry for 2 minutes until the fennel is golden. Add the white wine and allow to bubble until the wine is reduced by two-thirds. Return the pork to the pan, add the lemon rind and heat through for 2 minutes.

Sprinkle over the pine nuts. Add the pasta to the pan and stir until all the ingredients are well combined. Squeeze over the lemon juice. Serve with grated Parmesan and a drizzle of extra-virgin olive oil.

Spaghetti with pork, fennel and lemon

Herb pork sausages with gremolata

Zesty

Gremolata is an Italian seasoning made from fresh parsley and lemon, and is traditionally added at the end of stews and pasta dishes. It also works very well as a finishing touch to stir-fries.

Serves 3–4

1 Tbsp **peanut oil**
6 **spicy Italian sausages,** thickly sliced
2 **garlic cloves,** roughly chopped
10oz (300g) **spring greens,** finely shredded
1¾ cups (400g) canned **cannellini beans,** drained and rinsed
Salt and freshly ground black pepper, to season

For the gremolata:
2 **garlic cloves,** peeled
Grated rind and juice of 1 **lemon**
1 small bunch **flat-leaf parsley**
Salt and freshly ground black pepper, to season
2 Tbsp **extra-virgin olive oil**

Heat a large frying pan or wok and add the oil. Stir-fry the sausages for 5 minutes until they are golden brown. Add the garlic and stir-fry for a further 2 minutes.

Add the spring greens to the pan, along with the beans. Stir everything together and cook for a further 2 minutes until heated through. Season with salt and freshly ground black pepper.

To make the gremolata, mash 2 garlic cloves to a paste. Mix in the lemon rind and chopped parsley and season with salt and pepper.

Stir the gremolata mixture through the beans and squeeze over the lemon juice. Finish with a drizzle of extra-virgin olive oil.

Herb pork sausages with gremolata

Pork with spicy pears

Aromatic

This is an adaptation of a pear chutney I often make to go with cold meats and patés. The tartness, and also the sweetness, of the pear cuts perfectly through the richness of pork.

Serves 2–3

2 Tbsp **peanut oil**
1lb (450g) **pork tenderloin,** cut into thin strips
1 **large chilli,** deseeded and finely chopped
¼ cup (55g) **extra-fine sugar**
2 **garlic cloves,** finely chopped
2 **shallots,** peeled and finely diced
1 small glass **white wine**
4 **unripe pears,** peeled and cut into quarters
3 Tbsp **flat-leaf parsley,** chopped

Heat a large frying pan or wok and add 1 Tbsp oil. Add the pork and stir-fry in batches, for 5 minutes per batch, until golden. Set aside and keep warm.

Re-heat the pan and add the remaining oil. Add the chilli, sugar, garlic, shallots and wine, and stir-fry for 5 minutes until the wine has reduced by two-thirds. Add the pears and stir-fry for 3 minutes until the pears have softened but still keep their shape. Return the pork to the pan and stir-fry for 1 minute, sprinkle over the flat-leaf parsley and serve.

■ *Pork works well with many fruits, and pears are no exception. For an extra treat, crumble some Stilton or Gorgonzola cheese over the dish at the end of cooking.*

Pork with black bean and sweet chilli sauce

Distinctive

Black bean sauce is a popular Chinese marinade made from a blend of fermented black beans, spices, chillies and garlic. It has a rich and distinctive aroma and works well with richer meats.

Serves 4

2 Tbsp **black bean sauce**
1 Tbsp **sweet chilli sauce**
2 Tbsp **sesame oil**
2 Tbsp **peanut oil**
2 **carrots,** thinly sliced
1 **red pepper,** deseeded and cut into small chunks
scant ½ cup (75g) **snow peas,** finely sliced
1 **onion,** roughly chopped
10oz (300g) **pork tenderloin,** thinly sliced
2 Tbsp **sesame seeds,** toasted

To serve:
Noodles
Shredded green onions

In a bowl, whisk together the black bean sauce, sweet chilli sauce and sesame oil. Set aside.

Heat a large frying pan or wok and add 1 Tbsp oil. When the pan is hot and slightly smoking, add the carrot, pepper, snow peas and onion and stir-fry for 2–3 minutes. Remove from the pan and set aside. Clean the pan and re-heat it.

Add the remaining oil and stir-fry the pork in batches for 5 minutes. Pour in the sauce with 3 Tbsp water and cook for 2 minutes until the sauce has reduced. Return the carrot, pepper, snow peas and onion to the pan and heat through. Sprinkle over the sesame seeds and serve with noodles and shredded green onions.

Pasta with pancetta, mushrooms and pine nuts

Earthy

I always keep a piece of pancetta in the fridge. It lasts for ages and adds flavor to soups, stews, stir-fries and pasta sauces.

Serves 3–4

13oz (370g) **dried pasta, e.g. penne**
Olive oil, for sprinkling
10oz (300g) **pancetta**
1 Tbsp **peanut oil (optional)**
2 **garlic cloves,** finely sliced
6 cups (450g) **chestnut mushrooms,**
    cut into quarters
4 Tbsp **pine nuts,** toasted
4 Tbsp **chopped flat-leaf parsley**
4 Tbsp **shredded basil**
4 Tbsp **Parmesan cheese,** grated
2 Tbsp **extra-virgin olive oil,**
    for drizzling
Freshly ground black pepper,
    to season

Heat a large pan of lightly salted water. When boiling, add the pasta and cook for 10 minutes. Drain, sprinkle over a little olive oil to prevent sticking and set aside.

Heat a large frying pan or wok and add the pancetta. Stir-fry for 5 minutes until the pancetta is crisp. If the pan is dry, add a little peanut oil. Add the garlic and stir-fry for a further 1 minute.

Add the mushrooms and stir-fry for 5 minutes. Add the toasted pine nuts and cooked pasta and stir through until the ingredients are well combined.

Sprinkle over the parsley and basil and stir through the Parmesan cheese. Serve with a drizzle of olive oil and season with freshly ground black pepper.

■ *If you want to add a bit of a kick, add 1 tsp harissa paste or 1 red chilli, deseeded and finely sliced. Add to the pan with the pancetta.*

Pasta with pancetta, mushrooms and pine nuts

Red wine sausages with rosemary and lentils

Red wine sausages with rosemary and lentils

Comforting

Use good-quality pork sausages. Cheaper versions are full of bulking ingredients and water and have very little flavor. The best are made using free-range pork, with a meat content of around 80 percent.

Serves 3–4

1 Tbsp **olive oil**
6 **spicy Italian sausages**
2 **red onions,** finely sliced
2 **garlic cloves,** finely sliced
2 **celery sticks,** finely sliced
¼ cup (60ml) **red wine**
generous 1 cup (250g) **Puy lentils or green lentils,** cooked
4 Tbsp **passata**
1 sprig **fresh rosemary**
Salt and freshly ground black pepper, to season

To serve:
Crusty bread
Mixed salad

Heat a large frying pan or wok and add the oil. When the pan is slightly smoking, add the sausages and stir-fry for 5 minutes. Add the onions, garlic and celery and stir-fry for a further 5 minutes until golden.

Pour in the wine and boil until the liquid has reduced by two-thirds. Add the lentils, passata and rosemary and season with salt and freshly ground black pepper. Bring to a simmer and cook for 10 minutes.

Serve with crusty bread and a salad.

Hoisin pork in sherry

Savory

My daugher, Megan, loves hoisin sauce – in fact, she's crazy about all Chinese food. Hoisin is a barbecue sauce and works especially well with pork.

Serves 2–3

8oz (225g) **lean pork,** thinly sliced
4 Tbsp **hoisin sauce**
2 tsp **sesame oil**
2 Tbsp **dry sherry**
1 **garlic clove,** finely sliced
2 Tbsp **peanut oil**
generous 1½ cups (285g) **snow peas**
¾ cup (170g) **bean sprouts**

To serve:
Fried rice

Combine the pork, hoisin sauce, sesame oil, sherry and garlic in a medium-sized bowl. Cover and refrigerate for 30 minutes.

Drain the pork and reserve the marinade. Heat 1 Tbsp peanut oil in a large frying pan or wok. Stir-fry the pork until it is browned and cooked. Remove and keep warm.

Wipe the pan and add the remaining oil. Stir-fry the snow peas and bean sprouts for 3 minutes. Return the pork to the pan with the reserved marinade and bring to a boil and simmer for 2 minutes. Serve with fried rice.

Pork with red onion, orange and thyme

Delicious

The sweetness of the caramelized red onions contrasting with the bitterness of the orange makes a delicious and unusual variation on the traditional sweet and sour pork.

Serves 2–3

2 Tbsp **peanut oil**
10oz (300g) **lean pork,** thinly sliced
2 **red onions,** peeled and cut into
  quarters
1-in (2-cm) piece **fresh ginger,**
  peeled and finely chopped
2 **garlic cloves,** finely chopped
2 Tbsp **soy sauce**
Grated rind and juice of 1 **orange**
2 sprigs **fresh thyme or**
  1 tsp **dried thyme**

To serve:
Roasted new potatoes
Buttered spinach

Heat a large frying pan or wok and add 1 Tbsp oil. When the pan is smoking add the pork in batches and stir-fry for 5 minutes per batch. When all the batches are cooked, set the pork aside and keep warm.

Re-heat the pan and when hot add the onion and stir-fry for 5 minutes until golden. Add the ginger and garlic and stir-fry for a further 1 minute.

Add the soy sauce, orange rind and juice and the thyme. Cook for 2 minutes. Return the pork to the wok and stir-fry until the pork is heated through. Serve with roasted new potatoes and buttered spinach.

Fish dishes

I describe fish as nature's fast food. It's quick, nutritious and if prepared at its peak of freshness – absolutely delicious.

Included in this chapter are recipes from around the world, from a Goan shrimp curry (page 104) to Thai-style mussels (page 110) and a Mediterranean squid stir-fry (page 117). A huge variety of different fish and seafood are used, showing how versatile and impressive stir-fries can be.

Care has to be taken when stir-frying fish because of its delicate nature. A good way of protecting the flesh is to first coat the fish in a little flour and shake off the excess. It's also important not to be too vigorous when stir-frying or the flesh will break up.

Seafood is perfect for stir-frying and if you really want fresh, buy it live. I know this might sound a bit daunting, but I promise you'll notice the difference. Again, when buying shellfish always buy in season. There's nothing nicer than a stir-fry that has been whipped up using fresh and flavorsome ingredients.

Shrimp with garlic and chilli

Shrimp with garlic and chilli

Versatile

Once cooked, shrimp toughen easily and lose their lovely sweet flavor. So buy them raw and cook them until they change color.

Serves 4

2 Tbsp **peanut oil**
1 **red onion,** finely chopped
3 **garlic cloves,** finely chopped
1 **red chilli,** deseeded and
  finely sliced
24 **large raw shrimp,** deveined
  with the tails left on
2 **tomatoes,** roughly chopped
**Salt and freshly ground black
  pepper,** to season
1 small bunch **flat-leaf parsley,**
  roughly chopped
Extra-virgin olive oil, for drizzling

To serve:
Crusty bread

Heat a large frying pan or wok and add 1 Tbsp oil. Add the onion and stir-fry for 5 minutes. Add the garlic and chilli and cook for a further 1 minute. Add the shrimp and stir-fry for about 4 minutes until they turn pink and are cooked through. Turn into a bowl and set aside.

Re-heat the pan and add the remaining oil. When hot, add the tomatoes and stir-fry for 2 minutes. Season with salt and freshly ground black pepper. Return the shrimp to the pan and stir through. Scatter over the flat-leaf parsley and drizzle with olive oil.

■ *This dish works well on its own, served with chunks of garlic bread, or it can also be used as a pasta sauce for linguine or fine noodles.*

Goan shrimp curry
Fragrant

This creamy curry is characteristic of southern Indian cuisine. Fish and seafood are in abundance and are often cooked in creamy, coconut-based sauces.

Serves 3–4

For the garlic paste:
2 Tbsp **peanut oil**
2 **medium-sized onions**, finely sliced
2 **garlic cloves**, finely chopped
1 Tbsp **fresh ginger**, peeled and grated

1 Tbsp **tomato paste**
1 tsp **garam masala**
1 tsp **ground turmeric**
1 tsp **chilli powder**
5fl oz (150ml) **coconut cream**
24 **raw shrimp**, deveined with the tails left on

To serve:
Boiled rice

To make the garlic paste, heat a wok or a large frying pan. Add 1 Tbsp peanut oil and cook half the sliced onions until brown. Add the garlic and ginger, stir and remove from the heat. Cool the mixture, then blend to a paste in a food processor and reserve.

Wipe the pan and re-heat. Add the remaining oil and cook the remaining onions. Stir-fry for 5 minutes until translucent, then add the garlic and ginger paste. Stir-fry for 1 minute then add the tomato paste, garam masala, turmeric, coriander, chilli powder and coconut and bring to a boil.

Drop in the shrimp, bring back to a boil and then reduce the heat to a simmer. Stir-fry for 2–3 minutes and serve with boiled rice.

■ *As an alternative, replace the shrimp with scallops or pieces of firm white fish dusted in cornstarch.*

Fish in hot and sour sauce

Asian

The flour protects the delicate meat of the fish when you are cooking over a very high heat. It also helps to thicken the hot and sour sauce.

Serves 3–4

1 lb (450g) **firm white fish,** skinned and cut into 1-in (2.5-cm) strips
1 Tbsp **all-purpose flour,** seasoned with salt and freshly ground black pepper
¼ cup (70ml) **peanut oil**

For the hot and sour sauce:
¼ cup (70ml) **chicken stock**
1 Tbsp **dry sherry**
1 Tbsp **soy sauce**
2 tsp **tomato paste**
½ tsp **chilli powder**
1 Tbsp **white wine vinegar**
1 tsp **sugar**

2 **green onions,** finely sliced
1 small bunch **cilantro,** chopped

To serve:
Noodles

Dip the fish strips in the seasoned flour and shake off any excess. Heat a large frying pan or wok and add the oil. When it is really hot add the fish strips and stir-fry for 2–3 minutes until the fish is golden brown. You may have to do this in several batches, so remove each batch when it is ready and drain on paper towel and keep warm in the oven.

Pour off all the oil, wipe the pan clean and re-heat it. Add all the ingredients for the hot and sour sauce. Bring to a boil, then reduce the heat to a simmer for 5 minutes. Pour over the fish strips. Garnish with green onions and chopped cilantro and serve with noodles.

Cod with chilli soy vegetables

Cod with chilli soy vegetables

Tasty

Make sure you don't marinate this dish for too long. The acidity in the lemon will start to cook the fish.

Serves 4

For the marinade:
1 **red chilli,** deseeded and finely chopped
2 tsp **sesame oil**
Juice of 1 lemon
1 Tbsp **soy sauce**
1lb (450g) **firm white fish, e.g. cod or haddock,** skinned and cut into bite-sized pieces

For the stir fry:
2 Tbsp **vegetable oil**
1 **red chilli,** deseeded and finely chopped
1-in (2-cm) piece **fresh ginger,** peeled and grated
2 **garlic cloves,** finely sliced
½ cup (120g) **baby corn**
scant ½ cup (110g) **fresh or frozen peas**
scant ½ cup (110g) **bean sprouts**
2 **green onions,** finely sliced

To serve:
Toasted sesame noodles

In a medium-sized bowl mix the marinade ingredients together and add the fish. Cover and refrigerate for 5 minutes.

Heat a large frying pan or wok and add the oil. When it is hot, add the chilli, ginger and garlic, and stir-fry for 1 minute.

Add the baby corn, peas, bean sprouts and green onions and stir-fry for 2 minutes. Remove and keep warm. Re-heat the wok, remove the fish from the marinade and add to the pan. Stir-fry gently for a further 2 minutes until the fish is opaque and cooked through. Serve with the vegetables and toasted sesame noodles.

Thai ginger shrimp with lime

Tempting

This is quite a dry curry because I've only used a small amount of coconut milk. For a creamier curry you can easily add some more coconut milk to make a lovely sauce.

Serves 4

2 tsp **fresh ginger**, grated
1 Tbsp **fish sauce** (*nam pla*)
2 tsp **brown sugar**
4 **green onions**, finely sliced
24 **medium-sized raw shrimp**
1 **red chilli**, deseeded and finely chopped
1 **small onion**, finely chopped
2 **garlic cloves**, finely chopped
1 tsp **ground coriander**
2 Tbsp **peanut oil**
3 Tbsp **canned coconut milk**
Juice and zest of 1 **lime**
1 **red chilli**, finely sliced to garnish
4 Tbsp **fresh basil**, chopped to garnish

To serve:
Thai fragrant rice

In a small bowl, mix together the ginger, fish sauce, sugar and green onions. Marinate the shrimp in the mixture for 10 minutes.

Meanwhile, put the chillies, onion, garlic and coriander in a blender. Blend until the paste is well combined, scraping down the sides of the bowl if necessary.

Heat 1 Tbsp oil in a large frying pan or wok, add the paste mixture and stir-fry for 1 minute. Add the remaining oil and stir-fry the shrimp with their marinade for a further 3 minutes or until they change color. Add the coconut milk, lime zest and juice and stir for 1 minute until all the ingredients are well combined and heated through.

Sprinkle over the sliced chilli and fresh basil and serve with Thai fragrant rice.

Haddock with spicy beans

Warming

For really fresh haddock, look for translucent flesh that is firm to the touch. Smoked haddock can also be used as an alternative. Try and stay away from the scary, bright yellow variety and buy undyed.

Serves 4

2 Tbsp **peanut or vegetable oil**
2 **onions,** finely chopped
1 tsp **cumin seeds**
2 **garlic cloves,** finely chopped
1¾ cups (400g) canned **navy beans**
6 **plum tomatoes,** cut into quarters
Grated rind of 1 **lemon**
1 Tbsp **sweet paprika**
1 tsp **chilli powder**
1 Tbsp **tomato paste**
Salt and freshly ground black pepper, to season
4 **thick haddock fillets,** cut into bite-sized chunks
2 Tbsp **flat-leaf parsley,** chopped

To serve:
Mashed potatoes
Green salad

In a large frying pan or wok, heat the oil and add the onion and the cumin seeds. Stir-fry for 5 minutes until the onion is golden. Add the garlic and cook for a further 1 minute.

Add the beans, tomatoes, lemon rind, sweet paprika, chilli and tomato paste. Bring to a boil and simmer for 5 minutes and season with salt and freshly ground black pepper. Add the haddock, cover the wok and simmer for a further 5 minutes until the fish is opaque and just cooked. Sprinkle over the flat-leaf parsley and serve with mashed potatoes and a green salad.

Thai-style mussels

Exotic

Red curry paste is made from red chillies, shrimp paste and lemongrass, and is very popular in Thai cooking. Make sure your mussels are very fresh; discard any that stay open when tapped and any that fail to open when cooked.

Serves 4

2 **garlic cloves,** finely sliced
4 **green onions,** finely sliced
2lb (900g) **fresh mussels,** scrubbed
  and cleaned
3 Tbsp **Thai red curry paste**
¾ cups (150ml) **coconut milk**
Grated rind and juice of 1 **lime**
1 tbsp **fish sauce (*nam pla*)**
1 **small bunch cilantro,** roughly
  chopped

To serve:
Noodles

Put the garlic, green onions and 5fl oz (150ml) water in a large frying pan or wok. Bring the water to a boil, then add the mussels. Put a tight-fitting lid on the pan and cook for 2–3 minutes or until all the mussels are cooked and the shells are open. Discard any that stay shut. Drain the mussels through a sieve, reserving the cooking liquor, and set them aside.

Wipe the pan and pour in the mussel cooking liquor. Add the curry paste and coconut milk and bring up to a simmer. Put the mussels back into the pan with the lime rind and juice and the fish sauce. Cook everything for 1 minute, then stir in the cilantro. Serve with noodles.

Thai-style mussels

Scallops with minted green lentils

Scallops with minted green lentils
Summery

Bacon and scallops work brilliantly together. In the late spring I use delicious, fresh broad beans instead of lentils. Shelling the beans is time-consuming and a labor of love. However, the sweetness with the scallops makes it worthwhile.

Serves 3–4

2 Tbsp **olive oil**
12 **scallops,** with the corals on
4 strips **bacon,** cut into small pieces
2 **garlic cloves,** finely chopped
1¾ cups (400g) canned **green lentils**
1 bunch **flat-leaf parsley**
2 Tbsp **mint,** chopped
Juice of 1 **lemon**
4 Tbsp **extra-virgin olive oil**

Heat the oil in a large frying pan or wok. Cook the scallops in batches for 1 minute until golden on each side. Remove and set aside.

Re-heat the pan and add the bacon. Stir-fry for 2 minutes, then add the garlic and stir-fry for a further 1 minute until golden. Add the lentils, parsley and mint. Stir for 5 minutes until heated through.

Return the scallops to the pan and stir-fry gently to heat through, then serve with a squeeze of lemon and a drizzle of olive oil.

Crispy tuna with sweet chilli vegetables

Foolproof

This easy-to-make dish includes bok choy, a green leafy vegetable originally from China. Its slightly mustardy flavor makes it a delightful addition to stir-fries, soups and noodle dishes. Tuna is perfect for stir-frying as it holds its shape while cooking. Always use fresh tuna for this recipe and not canned.

Serves 4

1lb (450g) **tuna steak,** cut into bite-size chunks
2 tsp **cornstarch**
2 Tbsp **vegetable oil**
2 **red onions,** sliced
2 **red peppers,** finely sliced
2 small heads **bok choy**
1 Tbsp **soy sauce**
1 Tbsp **sweet chilli sauce**
1 Tbsp **lime juice**
2 tsp **honey**
1 small bunch **fresh mint,** roughly chopped

Toss the tuna in the cornstarch and shake off any excess. Heat a large frying pan or wok and add the oil. Stir-fry the tuna in batches, for 5 minutes per batch. When each batch is cooked, remove and drain on paper towel. Set aside.

Wipe the pan and re-heat. When hot and slightly smoking, stir-fry the onion and peppers for 5 minutes until soft. Add the soy sauce, chilli sauce, lime juice, honey and bok choy, and stir-fry for 1 minute until hot and the bok choy has wilted. Tip into a serving dish, top with the crispy tuna and scatter over the mint.

Crispy tuna with sweet chilli vegetables

Tuna with spinach and capers

Healthy

I love spinach and, in my opinion, stir-frying gets the best out of this wonderful green. To avoid over-cooking, simply fold in the spinach at the end of cooking.

Serves 3–4

2 Tbsp **peanut oil**
1 **large onion,** finely chopped
2 **garlic cloves,** finely chopped
1¼-in (3-cm) piece **fresh ginger,** peeled and grated
1 small glass **white wine**
1lb (450g) **tuna,** cut into bite-sized chunks
1 Tbsp **capers,** rinsed
6¼ cups (300g) **spinach,** washed
Salt and freshly ground black pepper, to season
2 Tbsp **extra-virgin olive oil,** for drizzling
1 **lemon,** cut into quarters

To serve:
Rosemary and garlic roast potatoes

Heat a large frying pan or wok and when hot, add the oil. Add the onion and stir-fry for 5 minutes. Add the garlic and ginger and stir-fry for a further 2 minutes.

Pour in the wine and simmer until there is only about 1 Tbsp remaining. Add the tuna and capers and gently stir-fry for a further 5 minutes. Fold in the spinach until it is wilted and season with salt and freshly ground black pepper.

Tip onto a plate and drizzle with the olive oil. Serve with lemon quarters for squeezing. Great served with rosemary and garlic roast potatoes.

Mediterranean squid stir-fry

Hearty

Try to get hold of young squid – they are more tender and benefit from quick cooking. Larger squid work better in slow-cook dishes.

Serves 4

2lb (900g) **squid,** cleaned and cut
   into thick rings
¼ cup (60ml) **sherry**
¼ cup (60ml) **lemon juice**
2 Tbsp **brown sugar**
2 **garlic cloves,** crushed
1 tsp **dried oregano**
2 Tbsp **olive oil**
2 **green onions,** finely sliced
2 **large red peppers**
2 **large yellow peppers**
4 **tomatoes,** roughly chopped
generous ¼ cup (85g) **black olives,**
   pitted
4 Tbsp **flat-leaf parsley**
**Salt and freshly ground black
   pepper,** to season

To serve:
Green salad
Crusty bread

In a large bowl, combine the squid, sherry, lemon juice, sugar, garlic and oregano.

Heat 1 Tbsp oil in a large frying pan or wok. Stir-fry the squid in batches, for 1 minute per batch, until tender. Remove from the pan and set aside.

Heat the remaining oil and stir-fry the green onions and peppers for 3 minutes, then add the tomatoes and cook for a further 2 minutes until softened.

Return the squid to the wok with the olives. Stir-fry until hot and cooked through. Garnish with the parsley and season with salt and freshly ground black pepper.

Cajun mackerel

Cajun mackerel

Healthy

Mackerel is an oily fish that people either love or hate. Personally, I think it is fantastic and very underrated. High in fish oils and Omega 3 fatty-acids, it's known as a superfood and is extremely good for you.

Serves 3–4

1 tsp **coriander seeds**
1 tsp **green peppercorns**
1 tsp **cumin seeds**
1 Tbsp **white wine vinegar**
2 drops **tabasco sauce**
2 drops **Worcestershire sauce**
8 **fresh mackerel fillets**
2 Tbsp **vegetable oil**
1 **red onion**, roughly chopped
6 cups (250g) **spinach**, washed
1¾ cups (400g) canned **black-eyed beans**
1 **lime**, for squeezing
2 Tbsp **virgin olive oil,** for drizzling

Grind the coriander seeds, peppercorns and cumin seeds in a small spice grinder or pestle and mortar and set aside.

Mix the vinegar, tabasco and Worcestershire sauce together in a small bowl and stir in the ground spices.

Make two diagonal cuts in each mackerel fillet and rub in the ground spice mixture. Let marinate in a cool place for 10 minutes.

Heat a large frying pan or wok and add 1 Tbsp oil. When hot, add the mackerel fillets and fry, without moving them, for 2 minutes. Gently turn over and continue frying for a further 2 minutes. Remove and set aside.

Re-heat the wok or frying pan and add the remaining oil. Stir-fry the onion for 2 minutes, then add the spinach and beans. Stir-fry for 2 minutes until the spinach is wilted and the beans are piping hot. Serve with the mackerel and squeeze over the lime and drizzle over the olive oil.

Quick kedgeree

Classic

This dish originated in Anglo-India, where it was traditionally eaten for breakfast. It also makes a good lunch or light dinner dish.

Serves 3–4

⅔ cup (150ml) **milk**
2 **bay leaves**
12oz (340g) **smoked haddock**
2 Tbsp **peanut oil**
4 **cardamom seeds,** crushed
1 Tbsp **garam masala**
2 tsp **turmeric**
1 tsp **ground coriander**
2 **cloves**
1 **onion,** finely chopped
½-in (1-cm) piece **fresh ginger,** peeled
   and grated
1 **green chilli,** deseeded and
   finely chopped
3¼ cups (285g) **cooked basmati rice**
2 Tbsp **fresh parsley,** chopped
**Salt and freshly ground black
   pepper,** to season

To serve:
2 **hard-boiled eggs,** shelled and cut
   into quarters
Lemon wedges

Put the milk in a pan large enough to hold the fish, then add the bay leaves and smoked haddock, bring to a simmer and poach for 5 minutes. Strain, cool and flake the fish into bite-sized pieces.

Heat a large frying pan or wok, add the oil, cardamom seeds, garam masala, turmeric, coriander and cloves. Stir-fry for 1 minute and then add the onion, ginger and chilli. Cook for a further 5 minutes. Add the cooked rice and stir well to combine all the ingredients.

Add the flaked fish, stir into the rice and cook for another 2 minutes until the fish is heated through. Scatter over the parsley and season with salt and freshly ground black pepper. Serve with the quartered hard-boiled eggs and lemon wedges.

■ *To cut down on the cooking time, replace the spices with a mild to medium curry paste.*

Quick kedgeree

Salmon with sun-blush tomatoes

Salmon with sun-blush tomatoes

Colorful

Sun-blush tomatoes are partly dried but do not have the same intense flavor of sun-dried tomatoes. If you can't get hold of sun-blush tomatoes and want to use sun-dried tomatoes instead, reduce the quantity by half.

Serves 3–4

3 Tbsp **olive oil**
2 **green onions,** finely sliced
2 **garlic cloves,** finely chopped
1lb (450g) **salmon,** skinned and cut into chunks
1¾ cups (400g) canned **cannellini beans**
Grated rind of 1 lemon
1 tsp **paprika**
¼ cup (55g) **sun-blush tomatoes,** roughly chopped
generous 2½ cups (125g) **wild arugula**
Salt and freshly ground black **pepper,** to season
Extra-virgin olive oil, for drizzling

Heat a large frying pan or wok and when hot add the oil. Add the green onions and garlic and stir-fry for 2 minutes, making sure you don't burn the garlic. Add the salmon and gently stir-fry the fish for 5 minutes. Remove, set aside and keep warm. Re-heat the pan and add the beans, lemon rind, paprika and sun-blush tomatoes. Stir-fry for 2 minutes until heated through.

Gently stir in the arugula and season with salt and freshly ground black pepper. Serve with fish and drizzle with a little extra-virgin olive oil.

Singapore noodles with salmon and shrimp

Leftover special

This is a good dish to make if you want to clear out the fridge and use up all the leftovers. If you don't have salmon, you can always use cooked chicken or tuna instead.

Serves 3–4

8oz (225g) **wide rice noodles**
1 **long red chilli**, deseeded and chopped
2 **garlic cloves**, crushed
½-in (1-cm) piece **fresh ginger**, grated and finely chopped
1 **small onion**, sliced
2 Tbsp **peanut oil**
12oz (340g) **salmon fillet**, skinned and cut into slices
12 **raw shrimp**, shelled
scant ½ cup (100g) **bean sprouts**
4 **green onions**, sliced
1 **egg**, lightly beaten
3 Tbsp **soy sauce**
Juice of 1 **lime**
1 small bunch **cilantro**, chopped

Put the noodles in a heatproof bowl, cover with boiling water and let soften for 7 minutes. Drain and set aside.

Meanwhile, put the chillies, garlic, ginger and onion into a food processor and process to a paste.

Heat the oil in a large frying pan or wok, add the paste and stir-fry for 30 seconds. Add the salmon and shrimp and stir-fry gently for 2–3 minutes until golden.

Add the drained noodles, bean sprouts, green onions and beaten egg and cook, stirring continuously, for 2 minutes. Pour in the soy sauce and lime juice and scatter over the chopped cilantro.

Salmon pilaf with saffron

Spiced

Saffron is the most expensive spice in the world. You might then think that using saffron for a quick stir-fry is a little extravagent. However, because the color and flavor are so intense, a little goes a long way.

Serves 4

2 Tbsp **peanut oil**
1lb (450g) **salmon fillet, skinned and** cut into large chunks
1 **onion,** finely chopped
4 **cardamom pods**
2 **cloves**
1 **cinnamon stick**
2 **bay leaves**
1 pinch **saffron threads**
⅔ cup (150ml) **vegetable stock**
3¼ cups (300g) **cooked basmati rice**
1 small bunch **cilantro**

Heat a large frying pan or wok and add 1Tbsp of the oil. When very hot add the salmon pieces and gently stir-fry for 2 minutes until the salmon turns an opaque color. Turn onto a plate, set aside and keep warm.

Wipe the pan and return to the heat. When hot, add the remaining oil and stir-fry the onion for 5 minutes until softened and golden. Add the cardamom, cloves and cinnamon, together with the bay leaves, and stir-fry for a further 2 minutes.

Add the stock, saffron and the cooked rice, combine well and stir-fry for 5 minutes. Discard the cinnamon stick and bay leaves, sprinkle the cilantro leaves over the dish and serve with the salmon.

■ *Basmati is the best rice for this dish as it has a low starch content and results in a light, fluffy rice. If you can't get hold of it you can use long-grain rice instead.*

Cod with chorizo and chickpeas
Spanish

Chorizo is a spicy Spanish sausage made with pork, cumin, garlic, red wine and lots of smoked paprika. You can buy fresh chorizo for cooking or dried for slicing and eating raw. I've used fresh for this recipe which imparts a deliciously intense flavor.

Serves 4

2 Tbsp **vegetable oil**
2 **red onions,** finely chopped
2 **garlic cloves,** finely chopped
2 **small chorizo sausages,** crumbled
1¾ cups (400g) canned **cooked chickpeas**
1¾ cups (400g) canned **tomatoes**
1lb (450g) **firm white fish, e.g. cod or haddock**
Juice of 1 lemon
Salt and freshly ground black pepper, to season
2 Tbsp **fresh cilantro,** chopped

To serve:
Rice or crusty bread

Heat a large frying pan or wok and add the oil. When hot add the onions and stir-fry for 5 minutes until golden. Add the garlic and stir-fry for a further 1 minute.

Add the chorizo, stir-fry for 2 minutes until golden then add the chickpeas and tomatoes. Bring to a simmer and add the fish. Cook for 3 minutes, stirring occasionally, until the fish is opaque and cooked. Add the lemon juice and season with salt and freshly ground black pepper. Sprinkle over the cilantro and serve with rice or crusty bread.

■ *Garlic mayonnaise is a perfect accompaniment to this hearty stew. Either serve it on your crusty bread or put a spoonful directly onto the stew.*

Cod with chorizo and chickpeas

Salmon, dill and fresh pea pasta

Salmon, dill and fresh pea pasta

Springtime choice

This is a wonderful late-spring dish, which can be served hot or cold. If you can't find young tender peas, replace with frozen peas or French beans.

Serves 3–4

12oz (340g) **dried spaghetti**
Olive oil, for sprinkling
2 Tbsp **vegetable oil**
2 **garlic cloves,** finely chopped
1lb (450g) **salmon fillet,** skinned and
    cut into chunks
1 cup (225g) **fresh or frozen peas**
1 small bunch **dill**
1 small bunch **mint**
4 **green onions,** finely sliced
Grated rind and juice of 1 **lemon**
2 Tbsp **extra-virgin oil,** for drizzling
4 Tbsp **Parmesan cheese,** to serve

Heat a large pan of lightly salted water. When boiling, add the pasta and cook for 8–10 minutes. Drain and run under cold water. Sprinkle with olive oil and set aside.

Heat the oil in a large frying pan or wok and add the garlic. Stir-fry for 30 seconds, making sure the garlic does not burn. Add the salmon and cook, without moving it around the pan, for 2 minutes. Turn the salmon over and cook for a further 2 minutes. Remove and keep warm.

Meanwhile, add the peas, pasta, dill, mint, green onions and lemon rind and mix well. Stir-fry for 2 minutes until heated through. Return the salmon to the pan. Sprinkle over the lemon juice and drizzle with olive oil. Grate over a little Parmesan.

Vegetarian delights

Stir-frying brings out the best in vegetables. It releases their flavor but retains their firm texture and essential nutrients.

I love vegetables, and as a seasonal cook I enjoy the excitement of seeing the first purple sprouting broccoli in February, perfect quickly stir-fried with a dash of soy sauce, sesame oil and garlic. And just when I start longing for something different, the first tender broad beans start appearing. Stir-fried with feta cheese, mint and pasta, they make a perfect spring supper.

Summer sees that start of an abundant crop of tomatoes, zucchini, and peppers – a heavenly summer combination along with pesto made with fresh summer herbs.

Autumn and winter move in and the days start to get longer. Wonderful golden squashes and root vegetables abound, which are ideal stir-fried and added to rice, making a fragrant autumn pilaf.

Tagliatelle with caramelized onions and walnuts
Robust

Tagliatelle are flat strips of pasta that are traditionally served with creamy sauces such as carbonara. I've used Gruyère cheese in this recipe instead of Parmesan because of its wonderful melting quality.

Serves 3–4

13oz (375g) **tagliatelle**
2 Tbsp **olive oil, plus** 1 tsp **for the pasta**
6 **large red onions,** finely sliced
2 **garlic cloves,** finely chopped
2 sprigs **rosemary,** chopped
1 small glass **white wine**
1 Tbsp **walnut oil (optional)**
1¼ cups (125g) **walnuts,** toasted and roughly chopped
3½oz (110g) **Gruyère cheese,** grated

Heat a large pan of lightly salted water. When boiling, add the pasta and cook for 8–10 minutes. Drain, stir in 1 tsp olive oil and set aside.

Heat a large frying pan or wok over a medium heat, add the olive oil and cook the onions over a moderate heat for 15 minutes. Add the garlic and rosemary and cook for a further 2 minutes

Pour in the wine and simmer until most of the wine has evaporated. Tip the pasta back into the red onion and toss well to mix everything. Stir in the walnut oil if using, followed by the walnuts and Gruyère.

■ *Try replacing the Gruyère with a blue cheese. The bitterness of the blue cheese works very well with the sweetness of the red onions.*

Tagliatelle with caramelized onions and walnuts

Tofu and vegetables in a honey teriyaki sauce

Meat alternative

Tofu is high in protein and makes a great meat substitute for vegetarians. It doesn't have any flavor so it benefits from marinating. Teriyaki sauce brings flavor to this dish and pairs well with the eggplants and mushrooms.

Serves 3–4

For the sauce:
1 Tbsp **honey**
2 Tbsp **teriyaki sauce**
Freshly ground black pepper, to season

2 Tbsp **peanut oil**
2 Tbsp **fresh ginger,** grated
2 **garlic cloves,** finely chopped
9oz (250g) **fresh tofu,** cut into bite-size chunks
4 **green onions,** thickly sliced
2 **eggplants,** cut into small chunks
4 **zucchini,** sliced thinly
6 cups (450g) **brown-capped mushrooms,** sliced
2 Tbsp **mint,** chopped
2 Tbsp **cilantro,** chopped

To make the sauce, put the honey and teriyaki sauce into a small bowl and mix. Season with freshly ground black pepper.

Heat a large frying pan or wok, add the oil, ginger and garlic and stir-fry for 1 minute. Add the tofu and stir-fry for a further 5 minutes. Remove and set aside. Reheat the wok, add the vegetables in batches and stir-fry for 5 minutes until brown and cooked through.

Add the dressing and stir through. Sprinkle with fresh mint and cilantro and serve.

■ *Depending on the size of your wok, heat the vegetables in batches to prevent them from boiling rather than stir-frying.*

Pasta with sweet and sour zucchini

Sicilian

This recipe was given to me by Nino, a Sicilian chef I used to work with. Golden raisins and pine nuts are a well-known combination in Sicilian cooking.

Serves 3–4

12oz (340g) **penne or any other short tube-shaped pasta**
2 Tbsp **olive oil, plus** 1 tsp **for the pasta**
8 **zucchini,** thinly sliced
2 **garlic cloves,** finely chopped
4 Tbsp **white wine vinegar**
1 Tbsp **extra-fine sugar**
⅓ cup (55g) **golden raisins**
½ cup (55g) **pine nuts,** toasted
4 Tbsp **Parmesan cheese,** grated

To serve:
Green salad

Cook the pasta in a large pan of boiling, lightly salted water for 8–10 minutes until cooked. Stir through 1 tsp olive oil and set aside.

Heat a large frying pan or wok and add the oil. Add the zucchini and cook for 5 minutes until they begin to soften. Add the garlic and cook for a further 2 minutes.

Add the vinegar and the sugar and let it bubble until almost evaporated. Add the raisins and pine nuts and stir through to combine all the ingredients. Add the cooked pasta and stir through once more. Sprinkle with Parmesan and serve with a green salad.

Pumpkin and sage pilaf

Pumpkin and sage pilaf

Sweet

This is a great dish in autumn when pumpkins are in abundance. It also makes a fantastic meal for vegetarians who will love the combination of flavors. You could also serve this as a side dish to a spicy curry.

Serves 4

3 Tbsp **peanut oil**
2lb (1kg) **pumpkin,** peeled and cut into bite-size chunks
4 **garlic cloves,** sliced
1 Tbsp **fresh sage,** finely chopped
3 cups (250g) **cooked basmati rice**
½ stick (75g) **butter**
1 tsp **ground nutmeg**
4oz (120g) **Parmesan cheese,** grated
Freshly ground black pepper, to season
Deep-fried sage leaves, to garnish

Heat a wok or a large frying pan. Add 2 Tbsp oil and stir-fry the pumpkin over a medium heat for 5 minutes. You may have to do this in batches depending on the size of your wok. Remove the pumpkin and keep warm.

Re-heat the pan and add the remaining oil. Add the garlic and cook for a further 1 minute until golden.

Add the pumpkin, cooked rice, butter and nutmeg and stir until all the ingredients are well combined and heated through. If the mixture is dry, add a little water. Sprinkle over the Parmesan, freshly ground black pepper and sage leaves and serve.

■ *To really bring out the sweetness in the pumpkin, roast in a medium oven with a drizzle of olive oil for about 15 minutes or until the pumpkin is tender.*

Indonesian vegetable curry

Unusual

I love to serve this curry as a warming winter meal. Its flavor and ingredients are different than a normal Asian stir-fry, making it a great conversation starter.

Serves 4

For the marinade:
1-in (2.5-cm) piece **fresh ginger,** finely grated
2 **red chillies,** finely chopped
2 **garlic cloves,** crushed
2 Tbsp **dark soy sauce**
1 Tbsp **brown sugar**
2 tsp **coriander seeds,** crushed
Juice of 1 **lime**
1lb (450g) **assorted vegetables,** e.g. carrots, zucchini, leeks, cut into equal sizes

For the curry:
2 Tbsp **peanut oil**
6 **green onions,** sliced thinly
2 Tbsp **light soy sauce**
1 small bunch **cilantro**
4 Tbsp **unsalted peanuts**

To serve:
Noodles

In a small bowl, mix all the ingredients for the marinade, add the vegetables and leave to marinate for 15 minutes in a cool place.

Heat a large frying pan or wok and add the oil. When the pan is hot and almost smoking, add the vegetables and stir-fry in batches, for 2–3 minutes per batch, until all the vegetable are browned.

Re-heat the pan and add the green onions and reserved marinade and continue to stir-fry for 2 minutes. Return the vegetables to the pan and continue to stir-fry for 2 minutes.

Add the light soy sauce and sprinkle over the fresh cilantro and peanuts. Stir through and serve with noodles.

■ *Cut all your vegetables to the same size and cook the denser vegetables first, or cook all the vegetables separately. This way you will guarantee that certain vegetables won't overcook.*

Cheesy leek and spinach pasta

Comforting

This is a real winter warmer. Try using a soft blue cheese for a different taste.

Serves 4

14oz (375g) **penne or similar short pasta**
Olive oil, for sprinkling
2 Tbsp **peanut oil**
2 **large leeks, total weight about 1lb (450g),** thinly sliced
1 small glass **white wine**
1 sprig **fresh rosemary**
1 sprig **fresh thyme**
4 Tbsp **heavy cream or crème fraîche**
1 Tbsp **wholegrain mustard**
4oz (125g) **mature Cheddar cheese**
generous 5 cups (225g) **baby spinach leaves**

To serve:
Green salad

Heat a large pan of lightly salted water. When boiling, add the pasta and cook for 10 minutes, then drain.

Meanwhile, heat a large frying pan or wok and add the oil. Add the leeks and stir-fry for 5–7 minutes until golden and soft. Add the white wine, rosemary and thyme and simmer until the wine reduces by two-thirds. Stir in the spinach, a handful at a time, until it wilts. If the mixture gets dry, add a little water. Add the cream or crème fraîche and mustard to the leeks and stir in the pasta and half the cheese. Stir in the remaining cheese and serve with a green salad.

Sweet chilli tofu and vegetable stir-fry

Flavorsome

Try to find unprocessed tofu, as it has a much better texture than cheaper processed tofu.

Serves 3–4

12oz (350g) **tofu**, cut into ¼-in (2-cm) cubes
1 Tbsp **light soy sauce**
1 Tbsp **sweet chilli sauce**
1 tsp **sesame oil**
2oz (50g) **egg noodles**
2 Tbsp **peanut oil**
2 **red peppers**, deseeded and roughly chopped
6 **green onions**, cut into 2-in (5-cm) slices
scant ¼ cup (85g) **snow peas**
1 Tbsp **cashew nuts**, roughly chopped
5 cups (225g) **bok choy**
2 Tbsp **soy sauce**

Put the tofu in a bowl with the soy sauce, sweet chilli sauce and sesame oil, and marinate for 30 minutes.

Cook the noodles in a large pan of salted boiling water for 4 minutes or until tender. Drain and run under cold water.

Heat a large frying pan or wok and add 1 Tbsp oil. When hot and slightly smoking, add the tofu and stir-fry for 2–3 minutes until golden. Remove and set aside.

Re-heat the pan and add the remaining oil. Add the peppers, green onions, snow peas and cashew nuts, and stir-fry for 3–4 minutes.

Return the noodles and tofu to the wok. Stir in the bok choy leaves. Stir-fry until all the ingredients are well combined and heated through, and the bok choy leaves are just cooked and wilted. Sprinkle with soy sauce.

Sweet chilli tofu and vegetable stir-fry

Sweet potato and broccoli stir-fry

Speedy

The red-fleshed variety of sweet potato is preferred for this dish. They're sweeter and less starchy, and combine well with the classic Asian soy and oyster sauces.

Serves 3–4

2 Tbsp **peanut oil**
2 **large sweet potatoes,** peeled and cut into bite-size chunks
4 **green onions,** thickly sliced
2 **red peppers,** deseeded and thinly sliced
8oz (225g) **broccoli,** cut into chunks
2 Tbsp **soy sauce**
4 Tbsp **oyster sauce**
2 Tbsp **sesame oil**
Toasted sesame seeds, to garnish

To serve:
Noodles

Heat a large frying pan or wok and add the oil. Add the sweet potato chunks and stir-fry for 5 minutes. Add the green onions, red peppers and broccoli and continue stirring for a further 5 minutes. If the pan gets dry, add a little water. Add the soy sauce and oyster sauce and allow to bubble for 2 minutes until reduced by half.

Sprinkle with sesame oil and toasted sesame seeds and serve with noodles.

Pasta with olives, artichokes and parsley

Hearty

Artichokes are one of the oldest known foods. They originated in the Mediterranean – Zeus was said to have turned a scorned lover into an artichoke! – but are now also grown in California. Artichoke hearts are the prize of the artichoke and are readily available in cans or jars, making them a great pantry staple.

Serves 3–4

12oz (375g) **dried spaghetti**
2 Tbsp **olive oil, plus** 1 tsp **for drizzling**
2 **red onions,** finely sliced
2 **garlic cloves,** finely chopped
2 cups (450g) canned **artichoke hearts,** drained and roughly chopped
½ cup (110g) **green olives,** pitted and roughly chopped
1 tsp **fresh thyme**
4 Tbsp **flat-leaf parsley,** roughly chopped
Freshly ground black pepper, to season
4 Tbsp **Parmesan cheese,** grated
Extra-virgin olive oil, for drizzling

Heat a large pan of lightly salted water. When boiling, add the pasta and cook for 10 minutes.

Meanwhile, heat a large frying pan or wok and add the oil. Add the onions and stir-fry for 5 minutes. Add the garlic and stir-fry for a further 1 minute. Add the artichokes, olives and thyme and stir-fry for 2 minutes.

Drain the pasta and add to the wok, then sprinkle over the flat-leaf parsley. Season with freshly ground black pepper. Sprinkle with the grated Parmesan cheese and serve with a drizzle of extra-virgin olive oil.

Quick ratatouille with mixed herb pesto

Quick ratatouille with mixed herb pesto

French

Ratatouille is a southern French vegetable stew of zucchini, eggplants and tomatoes, slowly cooked in tomato sauce. This is a stir-fry version with the addition of a homemade pesto sauce.

Serves 4

For the pesto:
1 small bunch **basil**
1 small bunch **mint**
1 small bunch **flat-leaf parsley**
6 Tbsp **olive oil**
1 **garlic clove,** roughly chopped
2 Tbsp **Parmesan cheese,** grated

2 Tbsp **peanut oil**
2 **garlic cloves,** crushed
6 **small zucchini,** finely sliced
1 **red pepper,** cut into quarters
1 **yellow pepper,** cut into quarters
1 **eggplant,** cut into small cubes
2 **red onions,** cut into quarters
4 **plum tomatoes,** cut into quarters
1 Tbsp **balsamic vinegar**
½ tsp **dried oregano**
2 Tbsp **pine nuts,** toasted
Basil leaves, to garnish

To serve:
Crusty bread

To make the pesto, whizz the herbs, olive oil and garlic in a food processor. Stir in the Parmesan and transfer the mixture to a bowl. Set aside.

Heat a large frying pan or wok and add the oil. Add the garlic and stir-fry for 1 minute. Stir-fry all the vegetables except for the tomatoes in batches, for 5 minutes per batch, and drain on paper towel. Repeat until all the vegetables are cooked.

Return all the vegetables to the pan and add the tomatoes, balsamic vinegar and oregano. Bring to a boil and simmer for 10 minutes. Sprinkle with toasted pine nuts and basil leaves and serve with the homemade pesto and chunks of crusty bread.

Penne with stir-fried tomatoes

Versatile

The success of this extremely quick tomato sauce is the sweetness of your tomatoes. If the sauce tastes a little bitter, add a little sugar.

Serves 4

12oz (375g) **dried penne**
4 Tbsp **olive oil**
1 **onion,** finely chopped
2 **garlic cloves,** finely chopped
15oz (425g) **cherry or baby plum tomatoes**
4 Tbsp **fresh basil,** finely shredded
4 Tbsp **Parmesan,** grated
Extra-virgin olive oil, for drizzling

Heat a large pan of lightly salted water. When boiling, add the pasta and cook for 8–10 minutes and drain.

Meanwhile, in a large pan or wok, add the olive oil and cook the onions over a medium heat for 5 minutes until opaque and soft. Add the garlic and cook for a further 2 minutes. Add the tomatoes and cook for 5 minutes.

Add the pasta to the pan and mix into the sauce. Sprinkle with the fresh basil and grated Parmesan, and serve with a drizzle of a good extra-virgin olive oil.

For a more substantial dish, add 5oz (150g) fresh buffalo mozzarella to the sauce.

■ *Fresh tomatoes give this dish a lovely flavor. If the tomatoes are not sweet, add a sprinkling of sugar.*

Butternut squash and feta pilaf

Autumnal

If butternut squash are not in season, zucchini make a lovely alternative and work wonderfully with feta.

Serves 3–4

2 Tbsp **olive oil**
2 **garlic cloves,** finely chopped
2 sprigs **thyme**
2 **red onions,** sliced into thin wedges
1lb (450g) **butternut squash,** peeled and cut into small cubes
2¾ cups (250g) **cooked long-grain rice**
¼ cup (60ml) **vegetable stock**
4oz (110g) **feta cheese,** crumbled
Salt and freshly ground black pepper, to season

Heat a large frying pan or wok and when hot add the oil. Add the garlic and thyme and stir-fry for 30 seconds until the garlic is golden. Add the onions and stir-fry for a further 5 minutes.

Add the butternut squash and stir-fry for 5 minutes. Add the cooked rice and stock, then stir-fry for 2 minutes until the rice is well heated through. Sprinkle over the feta and season well with salt and freshly ground black pepper.

■ *A serrated bread knife makes it easier to peel the squash. Add a few good-quality pitted olives, such as kalamata, for extra flavor if you wish.*

Pasta with mushrooms and chilli

Creamy

You can use any kind of cultivated mushroom for this dish. I like chestnut mushrooms as they have a firm texture and a deliciously nutty flavor.

Serves 3–4

12oz (340g) **dried short pasta,**
 e.g. penne
2 Tbsp **peanut oil**
3 **garlic cloves,** finely sliced
1 **red chilli,** deseeded and finely
 sliced
1 tsp **coriander seeds,** crushed
1lb (450g) **chestnut mushrooms,**
 sliced
1 small glass **white wine**
4fl oz (120ml) **heavy cream**
4 Tbsp **Parmesan cheese,** grated
4 Tbsp **flat-leaf parsley,** roughly
 chopped
Freshly ground black pepper,
 to season
Lime wedges

Heat a large pan of lightly salted water. When boiling, add the pasta and cook for 10 minutes.

Meanwhile, heat a large wok or frying pan and add the oil, garlic, chilli and coriander seeds. Stir-fry for 30 seconds. Add the mushrooms and stir-fry for a further 5 minutes. Add the wine and allow to bubble until it reduces by two-thirds. Stir in the pasta and double cream and heat through.

Sprinkle over the Parmesan, season with freshly ground black pepper and serve with a wedge of lime.

Pasta with mushrooms and chilli

Scrambled eggs with smoked salmon

Brunch choice

Make sure you use really fresh, free-range or organic eggs for this recipe. A lot of recipes suggest adding the smoked salmon to the eggs before cooking. I prefer not to do this as it cooks the smoked salmon, thus losing the subtle smokiness and tenderness.

Serves 4

8¾ cups (400g) **fresh spinach,** washed and dried
½ tsp **fresh nutmeg,** grated
Salt and freshly ground black pepper, to season
2 Tbsp **olive oil**
1 **small onion,** finely chopped
1 small bunch **basil,** roughly chopped
2 Tbsp **flat-leaf parsley,** chopped
12 **eggs**
1lb (450g) **smoked salmon**
1 large bunch **chives,** finely snipped
Freshly ground pepper, to season

To serve:
Lemon wedges
Buttered brown bread

Cook the spinach, using just the water clinging to the leaves after washing, for 3 minutes. Drain well, squeezing out as much liquid as possible. Add the grated nutmeg and season with salt and freshly ground black pepper. Roughly chop the spinach and set aside.

In a large non-stick frying pan or wok, heat the olive oil and cook the onion over a low heat for 5 minutes until it begins to soften. Add the spinach, basil and parsley and stir into the onion.

Lightly beat the eggs and add them to the spinach, stirring constantly. When the mixture is green and soft, remove from the heat and let stand for 2 minutes. Divide the smoked salmon between plates and serve the eggs on the side. Scatter over the chives. Season with freshly ground black pepper.

Serve with lemon wedges and slices of buttered brown bread.

Mushrooms with tarragon and crème fraîche

Easy

Mushrooms and tarragon are one of those combinations that just work. This dish is great as a pasta sauce or as an accompaniment to chicken.

Serves 4

2 Tbsp **peanut oil**
1 **large onion,** finely chopped
2 **garlic cloves,** finely chopped
1½lb (675g) **brown-capped mushrooms**
1 small bunch **tarragon,** chopped
½ cup (110g) **crème fraîche or sour cream**
Salt and freshly ground black pepper, to season
4 Tbsp **Parmesan cheese,** grated

To serve:
Baked potatoes
Poached eggs

Heat a large frying pan or wok and add the peanut oil. Stir-fry the onion for 5 minutes until golden, then add the garlic and stir-fry for a further 2 minutes. Add the mushrooms and stir-fry for 7–10 minutes until cooked.

Stir in the tarragon and stir-fry for 1 minute. Add the crème fraîche and season well with salt and freshly ground black pepper.

Sprinkle over the Parmesan cheese and serve with baked potatoes and poached eggs.

■ *For an early summer treat, replace the tarragon with sorrel.*

Fettucine with red beets and goat's cheese

Fettucine with red beets and goat's cheese

Pink

I used to make a soup, using roasted tomatoes and red beets, which was heavenly. I've used the same ingredients here and turned them into a quick stir-fry pasta dish. It's unusual but always loved!

Serves 4

14oz (400g) **dried penne pasta**
2 Tbsp **olive oil, plus** 1 tsp **for the pasta**
1 **large onion,** finely chopped
2 **garlic cloves,** crushed
12 **plum tomatoes,** cut into quarters
4 **large fresh red beets,** cooked and cut into wedges
1 tsp **fresh thyme**
2 Tbsp **basil,** roughly chopped
½ cup (110g) **black olives,** pitted and roughly chopped
Grated rind of 1 **lemon**
Salt and freshly ground black pepper, to season
4oz (110g) **soft goat's cheese**

Heat a large pan of lightly salted water. When boiling, add the pasta and cook for 8–10 minutes.

Meanwhile, in a large frying pan or wok, heat the olive oil over a medium heat. Add the onion and garlic and cook for 5 minutes until the onion has softened.

Add the tomatoes, red beets and thyme and stir-fry for 5 minutes. Stir through the basil, olives and lemon rind, then season with salt and freshly ground black pepper.

Stir in the pasta and continue to stir-fry for 2 minutes until all the ingredients are well combined. Serve with the goat's cheese.

Sweet suprises

I thought I'd throw in a few easy desserts that work wonderfully when stir-fried. Most of the desserts are fruit based and for true indulgence can be served with creamy ice-creams, warm pancakes and servings of plain yogurt or double cream.

As with vegetables, add fruits in order of their density and water content. Apples will take longer to cook than soft berries, and bananas only take moments.

Another thing to remember is not to overfill your wok. If necessary, cook the fruit in batches, otherwise you'll end up with fruit that has been stewed rather than stir-fried.

For a really healthy dessert option, omit using oil and add a couple of tablespoons of fruit juice instead. Heat to a simmer and add the fruit and stir-fry.

Have fun creating something sweet, delicious and unexpected using your stir-fry wok!

Bananas with honey and sesame seeds
Tasty

This is a twist on the classic Chinese deep-fried toffee bananas. It's easy to make and just as delicious.

Serves 4

¼ cup (55g) **sesame seeds**
2 Tbsp **honey**
4 **bananas,** peeled and cut in half

To serve:
Vanilla ice cream or plain yogurt

Heat a large frying pan or wok and add the sesame seeds. Toast them for about 30 seconds until browned, taking care not to burn them.

Add the honey and heat over a low heat until the honey is bubbling. Add the bananas and gently stir-fry for 30 seconds, making sure all the bananas are coated with the honey and sesame seeds.

Serve with vanilla ice cream or thick plain yogurt.

■ *This recipe works just as well with apples or pears.*

Bananas with honey and sesame seeds

Campari and orange stir-fry

Sophisticated

This is an ideal accompaniment for a sharp lemon sorbet or creamy vanilla ice cream.

Serves 4

5 **oranges,** peeled and divided into segments
2 Tbsp **brown sugar**
scant ½ cup (100ml) **Campari**

Heat a large frying pan or wok and add the orange segments and sugar. Stir-fry for 30 seconds. Add the Campari and stir until the liquid has reduced by half – this will take about 30 seconds. Serve immediately.

■ *Oranges also marry perfectly with the liqueur Cointreau.*

Oranges and almonds with Grand Marnier

Subtle

For a non-alcoholic version, replace the orange-flavored Grand Marnier liqueur with orange juice.

Serves 3–4

4 **oranges,** peeled and cut into quarters
2 Tbsp **soft brown sugar**
2 Tbsp **Grand Marnier**
½ cup (55g) **almonds,** toasted

To serve:
Pancakes
Plain yogurt

Heat a large frying pan or wok and when hot add the oranges, sugar and Grand Marnier. Stir-fry for 5 minutes until the sugar has dissolved and the oranges are hot and cooked through. Scatter over the almonds and serve with pancakes and plain yogurt.

Apple, raisin and cinnamon stir-fry

Spiced

This is delicious with a splash of Calvados, the classic apple liqueur from northern France.

Serves 4

½ stick (55g) **lightly salted butter**
4 **firm apples,** cored and sliced into thin segments
⅓ cup (55g) **raisins**
scant ¼ cup (25g) **extra-fine sugar**
1 level tsp **ground cinnamon**

To serve:
Vanilla ice cream or cream

Heat a large frying pan or wok and add the butter. When the butter has melted and has just begun to foam, add the apples. Stir them around, coating the segments in butter, and heat them for 1 minute.

Add the raisins and continue to stir for a further 2 minutes. Mix the sugar and cinnamon together and sprinkle over the apple and raisins. Stir all the ingredients together for 30 seconds, then serve immediately with vanilla ice cream or cream.

■ *This makes a delicious breakfast served with toasted brioche bread, a drizzle of honey and some plain yogurt.*

Apples and blackberries in a cassis syrup

Apples and blackberries in a cassis syrup

Autumnal

Crème de Cassis, a sweet, blackcurrant-flavored liqueur, is made from blackcurrants crushed into refined alcohol, with sugar subsequently added. Combined with white wine, it makes the classic French apéritif Kir.

Serves 4

2 Tbsp **peanut oil**
8 **apples,** cored, peeled and cut
  into quarters
⅔ cup (150g) **blackberries**
4 Tbsp **apple juice**
2 Tbsp **honey**
2 Tbsp **Crème de Cassis**
Fresh mint, to garnish

To serve:
Crème fraîche or sour cream
Pancakes

Heat a large frying pan or wok and, when hot, add the oil. Add the apple quarters and stir-fry for 2 minutes.

Add the blackberries, apple juice, honey and Crème de Cassis and continue to stir-fry for 4 minutes until the apples begin to break down and the sauce reduces to a syrup.

Sprinkle with mint and serve with crème fraîche or sour cream on pancakes.

Apricot and almond stir-fry

Luscious

Look for ripe, sweet apricots. If they are not ripe, increase the amount of sugar to 3 Tbsp.

Serves 3–4

½ cup (55g) **almonds**
½ stick (55g) **butter**
10 **apricots**
2 Tbsp **soft brown sugar**

To serve:
Vanilla ice cream

Heat a large frying pan or wok and add the almonds. Stir-fry for 1 minute until they start to turn golden brown. Add the butter and when this has melted add the apricots. Stir-fry all the ingredients for a further minute.

Sprinkle over the sugar and stir for 30 seconds. Serve with vanilla ice cream.

Summer berry stir-fry

Summery

This is a great way of making a quick and light dessert. You can also serve it as a sauce with ice-cream.

Serves 3–4

1¼ cups (100g) **redcurrants**
⅔ cup (200g) **strawberries**
⅔ cup (200g) **raspberries**
2 Tbsp **extra-fine sugar**

To serve:
Vanilla ice-cream

Heat the wok and add the redcurrants and heat for 30 seconds. Add the strawberries and stir for a further 30 seconds. Add in the raspberries and stir for 1 minute. Add the sugar, stir well and then serve with whipped cream.

Mango, pineapple, banana and lime stir-fry

Tropical

Make sure the fruit you stir-fry is fresh. Canned fruit is too soft and ends up boiling rather than stir-frying.

Serves 4

½ stick (55g) **butter**
1¼ cups (300g) **pineapple,** cut into chunks
1 **mango,** peeled, pitted and sliced
Juice of 1 **lime**
2 **bananas,** peeled and cut into chunks
1 Tbsp **extra-fine sugar,** for sprinkling
2 Tbsp **mint,** roughly chopped

To serve:
Plain yogurt

Heat a large frying pan or wok and add the butter. When it has melted, add the pineapple, stir for 30 seconds, then add the mango and stir for 1 minute. Add the lime juice to the wok and coat the fruit with it. Add the banana chunks and stir for 1 minute. Sprinkle with extra-fine sugar and mint. Serve with plain yogurt.

Poached pears with star anise

Intense

This recipe works better with under-ripe pears. Choose a firm variety that have an intense fragrance.

Serves 4

1 Tbsp **butter**
4 **pears,** cored and cut into quarters
2 Tbsp **brown sugar**
1 small glass **red wine**
1 **cinnamon stick,** broken
1 **star anise**
2 **cloves**

To serve:
Butterscotch
Ice cream

Melt the butter in a large frying pan or wok. Add the pears and the sugar and stir-fry for 2 minutes until the pears are golden. Remove and set aside.

Add the wine, cinnamon, cloves and star anise. Bring to a simmer and cook for 10 minutes until the red wine reduces by two-thirds and the pears are cooked.

Remove the pears from the cooking liquor and set aside. Increase the heat under the pan and boil the sauce for 5 minutes until it becomes syrupy. Pour over the pears and serve with butterscotch or ice cream.

Poached pears with star anise

Quick summer pudding

Cheat's version

This is a delicious alternative to bread pudding if you are in a hurry. Serve on a toasted sweet bread such as brioche and let soak for 10 minutes before serving.

Serves 4

½ cup (110g) **extra-fine sugar**
2 Tbsp **blackcurrant juice,** diluted
1 cup (225g) **strawberries,** hulled and cut into quarters
1 cup (225g) **blueberries**
1 cup (225g) **redcurrants**

To serve:
Brioche slices, toasted
Whipped cream

Heat a large frying pan or wok and add all the sugar and fruits. Stir-fry for 5 minutes until the fruit begins to break down. Pour the mixture over slices of toasted brioche and serve with a dollop of whipped cream.

Rhubarb and orange with ginger cream

Classic combination

Rhubarb is used to make a variety of tart sauces that can be eaten with desserts, or with pork and other fatty meats and game. Rhubarb goes particularly well with ginger.

Serves 4

2 Tbsp **orange juice**
1lb (450g) **rhubarb,** tops removed
    and sliced
1 tsp **ground ginger**
2 Tbsp **soft brown sugar**

For the ginger cream:
½ tsp **ground ginger**
4 Tbsp **heavy cream**

Heat a large frying pan or wok and add the orange juice. Bubble for 1 minute until reduced by half. Add the rhubarb, ginger and sugar, and stir-fry for 5 minutes until the rhubarb is soft and cooked through.

In a small bowl, mix the ginger with the heavy cream and serve with the rhubarb.

On the side

Perfect steamed rice

Serves 4–6

3 cups (400g) **long-grain rice**
2½ cups (600ml) **water**

Wash the rice until the water becomes clear. Drain and put in a heavy pan with the water and bring to a boil. Boil for about 5 minutes until most of the surface liquid has evaporated. Cover the pan with a tight-fitting lid, turn the heat as low as possible and let the rice cook, undisturbed, for 15 minutes. Let the rice rest for 5 minutes before serving.

Spicy potato mash

Serves 4

3 Tbsp **sunflower oil**
1 tsp **mustard seeds**
1 **green chilli,** chopped
4 **potatoes,** boiled, peeled and mashed
Salt, to season
4 Tbsp **fresh cilantro,** roughly chopped

Heat a wok until very hot and add 1 Tbsp of the oil. Add the mustard seeds. When they pop, add the chilli and stir. Add the mashed potatoes and season with salt. Blend well and allow to heat through. Remove and keep hot.

Serve the potatoes topped with fried onions and roughly chopped cilantro.

Stir-fried broccoli

Serves 4

1lb (450g) **broccoli or purple sprouting broccoli**
1 Tbsp **peanut oil**
2 **garlic cloves,** peeled and sliced
2 Tbsp **soy sauce**

Cut and slice the stems of the broccoli and break the head into even-sized florets. Use purple sprouting broccoli in whole pieces. Heat a wok over a high heat and add the peanut oil. When it is very hot and slightly smoking, add the garlic. Stir-fry for 30 seconds until the garlic is lightly browned.

Add the broccoli and stir-fry for 1 minute. Add the water, cover with a tight-fitting lid and cook over a high heat for 5 minutes or until the broccoli is tender and cooked. Uncover and sprinkle over the soy sauce to serve.

Couscous with mint and toasted almonds

Serves 4

2 cups (250g) **couscous**
2½ cups (570 ml) **hot chicken stock**
4oz (55g) **toasted almonds**
Salt and freshly ground black pepper, to season
1 small bunch **fresh mint,** chopped
1 small bunch **flat-leaf parsley,** chopped
Grated zest of 1 lemon

Place the couscous in a bowl and pour over the hot stock. Stir with a fork, cover with a cloth and allow to stand for 5 minutes.

Heat a frying pan or wok over a medium heat. Add the couscous and stir to break up the grains. Season with salt and freshly ground black pepper. Stir in the almonds, herbs and lemon zest and serve.

Green pea stir-fry

Serves 4

2 Tbsp **sunflower oil**
½ tsp **cumin seeds**
1 tsp **mustard seeds**
2 cups (300g) **frozen peas**
1 tsp **sugar**
3 Tbsp **desiccated coconut**

Heat the oil in a wok and add the cumin seeds and mustard seeds. Stir-fry for 30 seconds. Add the peas and stir. Pour in 4 Tbsp water, add the sugar and salt and stir-fry for 5 minutes until the peas are cooked through. Remove from the heat, stir in the coconut and serve.

Red onion and cardamom pilaf

Serves 4

2 Tbsp **oil**
5 **cardamom pods**
2 tsp **coriander seeds**
1 **large red onion**, finely chopped
generous 3 cups (450g) **basmati rice**, washed

In a large saucepan, heat the oil and add the cardamom and coriander seeds. Add the onion and stir-fry until the onion is lightly browned. Stir in the rice and cover with 2½ cups (600ml) water. Bring to a simmer, reduce the heat and cover. Cook for about 10 minutes. Let stand for a further 5 minutes without removing the lid. Fluff the rice up with a fork and serve.

About the author

Katie Rogers was trained as a chef at Leiths School of Food and Wine in London. After freelancing for five years as a chef, she became a food editor and food director for several magazines. Katie is particularly interested in local, seasonal and sustainable food. She has created and taught classes in fishing, preserving, and meat preparation. Currently she works as a food writer and stylist.

Index